College Entrepreneur Handbook

Ideas for a College Based Business

Jonathan R. Aspatore

OASIS PRESS

The Oasis Press® / PSI Research
Central Point, Oregon

Published by The Oasis Press®
© 1999 ebrandedbooks.com, Inc., a subsidiary of
Entrepreneur Products & Services LLC

This publication is designed to provide accurate and authoritative information
in regard to the subject matter covered. It is sold with the understanding that
the publisher is not engaged in rendering legal, accounting, or other professional service. If legal advice or other expert assistance is required, the services of a competent professional person should be sought.
> — *from a declaration of principles jointly adopted by a committee of
> the American Bar Association and a committee of publishers.*

Editor: Janelle Davidson
Book and Graphics Designer: Constance C. Dickinson
Typographer: Jan Olsson
Cover Designer: Steven Burns

Please direct any comments, questions, or suggestions regarding this book to
The Oasis Press®/PSI Research:

> Editorial Department
> P.O. Box 3727
> Central Point, OR 97502
> (541) 479-9464
> info@psi-research.com *email*

The Oasis Press® is a Registered Trademark of Publishing Services, Inc.,
an Oregon corporation doing business as PSI Research.

Aspatore, Jonathan Reed.
    College entrepreneur handbook : ideas for a college based
business / Jonathan R. Aspatore.
    p.   cm.
  Includes bibliographical references.
  ISBN 1-55571-503-6 (pbk.)
  1. New business enterprises. 2. Entrepreneurship. 3. College
students—Employment. I. Title.
  HD62.5 .A848 1999
  658.1'141—dc21
                                                            99-32991

Printed in the United States of America
First edition 10 9 8 7 6 5 4 3 2 1

♲ Printed on recycled paper when available.

For Rachel, who gives me the drive to succeed and the love to survive.

Table of Contents

Part III – Financial, Legal, and Tax Issues

Part IV – Quick Reference Guide

Acknowledgments

Special thanks go to Michael Mathews, Eli Burstein, Neil Sheth, Josh Klenoff, Lenny Chang, Josh Rappoport, Jonathan Kleiman, Lee Cantor, Judy Galani, and Ami Plasse for all of their help, support, and contributions.

About the Author

Jonathan R. Aspatore is the founder of EPS Business Partners (www.epsbp.com), which provides entrepreneurial solutions to companies worldwide. He has written numerous books on entrepreneurial thinking and new business development in addition to being a monthly columnist for numerous web sites and publications. Jonathan began his career with Morgan Stanley in New York after studying entrepreneurial management in the Wharton School of Business. After working as an Investment Banker in the technology sector and in the Derivatives Product Group at Morgan Stanley, he went on to start EPS Business Partners in 1997. As CEO of EPS, Jonathan has assisted numerous multimillion-dollar companies and start-ups assess and execute new business endeavors. For any comments, questions, or speaking opportunities, please contact him at: aspatore@epsbp.com

Introduction

College is a great time to start a business because you are surrounded with incredible resources and it is a good time to experiment with different opportunities. Starting a business teaches you how to think like an entrepreneur, a skill that will be useful the rest of your life, no matter what your career path.

Starting your own business is not as hard as you may think. With a Web site, e-mail address, and a product or service, you are well on your way to starting a successful and profitable business. Even though you may not have all of the necessary resources available to you, there is rarely a time when anyone starts a business under perfect conditions. The most important aspect of being an entrepreneur is to always believe in your ideas and yourself.

Use your time at college to experiment with entrepreneurial opportunities and learn from the invaluable lessons that entrepreneurship teaches. You never know, maybe you will have the success of such college entrepreneurs as Michael Dell of Dell Computers or Tom and Tom of Nantucket Nectars.

Good luck!

Part I

The Collegiate Entrepreneurial Perspective

Challenges of Starting a Business

The Entrepreneurial Process

Chapter 1

Challenges of Starting a Business

You must not give up if you are willing to take the risk.

Todd Krizelman and Stephan Paternot
Founders of theglobe.com

Entrepreneurship

Entrepreneurship can be one of the most gratifying experiences in business. An entrepreneur must learn every aspect of a business to be successful and find ways to be creative with limited resources. Very rarely do entrepreneurs begin with sufficient resources to make a dominant impact on an industry. Entrepreneurs use their limited resources in creative ways to give them a comparative advantage over their competitors.

College campuses are a great environment to start a business, and your college years are a good time to experiment with entrepreneurship. Being in college, you have an inside view and understanding of the collegiate marketplace. With a captive target market and insight on college trends nationwide, you can take advantage of upcoming markets and new concepts.

College students represent a dynamic part of the population, in addition to being future adult consumers. Large corporations often try to test market their new products and services in a college setting to see if they will be successful. Although these large companies have millions of dollars to spend on research and development, they lack the grass roots approach necessary to truly capitalize on college campuses. This represents a fantastic opportunity for you to take advantage of your first-hand knowledge to develop an idea into a profitable business.

College campuses are contained communities that thrive on the products and services offered within them. By capitalizing on a new product or service, you have an excellent opportunity to make money and to learn about running your own business. Whether you choose to conduct business exclusively on your college campus or you apply your talents to the marketplace as a whole, the college experience will expose you to all sorts of new opportunities. By meeting people, being in a new setting, and taking a wide range of classes, college naturally exposes you to a variety of experiences.

Entrepreneurship is a state of mind in which entrepreneurs learn to use their limited resources in a creative way to effectively maximize their talents and compensate for their weaknesses. This effective use of talents allows entrepreneurs not only to gain an advantage over much larger competitors but also to eventually create their own niche in the marketplace. College is an excellent time to begin thinking like an entrepreneur and to take a chance on starting your own business. Most people do not realize that Federal Express, Dell Computers, Nantucket Nectars, and many others were founded by college students.

➡ What skills do you have that will be valuable as an entrepreneur?
➡ What skills do you wish to develop from the entrepreneurial process?
➡ How would you define an entrepreneur?

The Decision Process

It is very important to evaluate carefully the positives and negatives to opening your own business. The thrill of building a business and making money is a wonderful feeling of accomplishment; however, to make that happen will require a lot of time and hard work. While running a business at college is a lot of additional work, by allocating the workload with friends and creating a niche for your business, it is possible for you to make your company a huge success and still meet your academic goals. Besides, wouldn't you rather run your own business and set your own hours than work at the local deli or cafeteria?

You must carefully consider the type of business that you want to start. Market timing and execution are critical in making your business a success. Some businesses are extremely successful offering their services only at certain times of the year while others rely on having their business continually up and running.

Map out personal and business goals for yourself and your company. Establish a timeline that you will use as a benchmark to make sure you keep on track. Decide how much time you want to spend on your business per week and whether it will require working with other individuals.

Do not be intimidated by others who claim how hard it is to start a business. If you can come up with a good idea and have the desire to succeed, the rest will fall into place. Making the decision to become an entrepreneur is not an easy one, but if you are a hard worker and a creative thinker with the will to succeed, you will find it to be an incredibly rewarding experience.

➡ Is it the proper time to be opening your business?

➡ What will be your comparative advantage over your competitors?

➡ Why do you want to become an entrepreneur?

➡ What do you think it will take to become a successful entrepreneur?

➡ What can you learn from people you know who have started their own business?

Time and Resource Commitment

It is important to decide what sort of time and resource commitment you are willing to put into your business. Different sorts of businesses require different amounts of time devoted to them. First identify whether you want to offer a product or a service. If offering a service, you must be available during the business hours you are open. By developing a product, you often have more flexibility to create your own schedule. Maybe your business relies solely on sales generated on your online store, or instead maybe you need to have people answering phones ten hours a day. Depending on your company's needs, you may have to get other people to work with you so you can share some of the time commitment. Even if you can do everything yourself, it is often very beneficial to have different perspectives on things and an extra person to help as the workload increases.

If you open a virtual store on the World Wide Web, your time commitment will be very different than if you open a service business that is time sensitive, such as a late night delivery service. Make sure to understand the time commitment your new business will require. If you get in over your head, it may take too much time away from other activities you need to focus on, such as academic and social activities.

Entrepreneurship is excellent for enhancing your time management skills because you are forced to perform a plethora of tasks within set time periods. This forces you to manage your time in an efficient manner so you can find time for your schoolwork, friends, and your new business. Many people find it easier to be more productive and actually feel better about themselves when they have a lot going on and are forced to manage their time effectively. By learning to maximize your time, you will accomplish more tasks than you ever thought possible.

Make sure that the business does not monopolize too much of your time, however. College is about having a lot of different experiences, and no one of those should entirely absorb your time and cause other areas to slip as a result. Unless your business shows the potential to be the next Dell Computers or Federal Express, you should not let it take over your life at college.

It is also important to assess the risk to you and your business on a financial level. If you are using your own money to finance your business, it is important to ensure that this will not dip into money that you need to live on at college. Money invested in your own business should be funds that can be tied up for quite some time. The return on investment from starting a business can often take months or even years. Be aware of this, and allocate enough funds to start your business and to help it run in the first months.

Starting a business can be very time consuming, and if you have a lot of other activities, you may want to find a couple of partners to help share the workload. But before anyone invests any money in your business, be sure to find out what they are expecting from your venture.

➡ How much time do you have to devote to a business on a weekly basis?

➡ What resources are available to you that would help you to start a business?

➡ What professors or other human resources are available on campus to consult with you?

➡ How will you start a business and still have time for everything else in your schedule?

Main Points

The challenges of starting a business are extensive; however, the rewards can be well worth the effort on many levels. Consider the following points before starting your business.

- Starting a business is never easy, yet the lessons learned make it an invaluable experience.
- Starting a business requires desire, focus, and the ability to listen and learn.
- Successful entrepreneurs take advantage of the resources around them to create a network of individuals to assist their company.
- Entrepreneurs are individuals who capitalize on opportunities in the marketplace.
- College is a good time to experiment with starting a business.

Get started by working out your thoughts with the time commitment analysis worksheet at the end of this chapter.

Interview

College Entrepreneurs Todd Krizelman and Stephan Paternot Owners of theglobe.com, interviewed by the author, June 5, 1998

Q: Tell me about your backgrounds.

A: We met while we were juniors at Cornell University in 1994. Todd originates from the Bay area of San Francisco and majored in biology. I moved from London and studied computer science and business.

Q: Tell me a little about your business.

A: theglobe.com is a leading Web community that seeks to replicate society through its active population of more than 6 million users and 1.8 million members. Members express their creativity with home-page building, discussion forums, e-mail, special interest groups, celebrity chat events, and live conferences on topical issues. The company is based in New York City, with an affiliate office in San Francisco, and just went public in 1998.

Q: How did you get interested in entrepreneurship?

A: The venture started off spontaneously while we were brainstorming in our dorm room. We had been discussing the huge potential of the Internet for an online community and decided to explore the concept further.

Q: What do you feel is the most challenging aspect of starting and owning your own business?

A: The company grew at a fast rate, from a staff of two to over 60 employees in under two years. We had to set up employee policies and deal with human resource issues such as vacation time and sick days. After graduating from college, this was quite a new challenge for us. Today, almost four years later, we have almost 100 employees.

Q: What do you find is the most rewarding aspect?

A: Remembering where we started from and experiencing where we are today. Having the opportunity to go after our dream and make it a reality.

Q: What resources do you find are helpful when starting a business?

A: An extremely valuable resource are the insights into the business world which we receive from our investors who played an important role in advising us with managerial decisions. Additionally, the support and encouragement we received from friends and family.

Q: What are your general thoughts on entrepreneurship?

A: If someone feels strongly about starting their own business, they must be willing to put 100 percent of a commitment into it. A person should also be prepared to experience some pitfalls and realize that these obstacles help them learn and will shape their business experience for success.

Q: What advice would you give younger people, specifically college students, on entrepreneurship and starting their own business?

A: One of the key elements of entrepreneurship is that you are taking a risk. The way to make it safer is to do as much preliminary research as possible about your industry and to speak with people who already have the experience of owning and operating a business.

We learned on the fly. We were college students without any managerial expertise, but we put in 14- to 16-hour days seven days a week and made the company a part of our life. We were very aggressive when we sold the concept of the business, even without a brand name. This was especially difficult when we approached investors. We wanted to be selective about who we would turn to for business advice and support at the beginning. There was not always an immediate reaction for them to embrace the idea.

You must not give up if you are willing to take the risk. Even if the business venture does not succeed immediately, and most don't, you have to stay focused and continue to plug away. As long as you are responsible in your preparation and stay committed to the business, the experience itself will prove to be worth your while.

Time Commitment Analysis

Time Estimate

Current available hours per week   _____

Hours you want to spend on your business   _____

Different tasks your business will require each week

_____   _____

_____   _____

_____   _____

_____   _____

_____   _____

_____   _____

Total hours your business will require each week   _____

Additional members you will need to hire

_____   _____

_____   _____

_____   _____

Notes _____

_____

_____

_____

_____

_____

_____

_____

_____

_____

_____

_____

_____

_____

_____

_____

_____

_____

_____

_____

_____

_____

_____

Chapter 2

The Entrepreneurial Process

The uncertainty of survival, the new challenges that an entrepreneur faces each day, and the long hours spent in creating something new are experiences that a successful entrepreneur will carry with them for the rest of their life.

Sabeer Bhatia
Founder of Hotmail Corporation

Reasons for Starting a Business

Because students in college have different ambitions, you should identify early on what you want to get out of your business. Map out goals for your business and a strategy for reaching them. The best way to do this is to make a timeline for your business. Be realistic in setting dates for tasks you want to have completed. Creating a timeline will help assure that you stay on course, not get too delayed at any point, and will keep you motivated and focused on perpetually making progress.

Include both your personal and business goals for starting a business. These should cover strategic, financial, and other goals. While your personal goals may not matter to your potential lenders or investors, they do matter to you and your company. Deciding to be an entrepreneur can have great effects on your life and the lives of those around you. Discuss these with your family and friends to get their feedback.

➡ What are your goals and objectives?
➡ What are your future plans for your business?
➡ What are your expectations for your business?

Identifying and Assessing the Opportunity

Entrepreneurs see opportunity where others see problems. Opportunities exist everywhere in the marketplace, so keep your eyes open at all times. You never know when you may come up with the next great business idea; it could be in bed, at a party, or even while you are studying.

As soon as you have decided what type of business you want to start, you must determine whether it is a profitable market for you to enter. Although an idea may sound great at first, some types of businesses are very difficult to make money in. One of the best ways to ensure that your business will hit the ground running is to test the waters and see if other people would use your product or service. These people then may actually become some of your first customers, giving your business the first push and the credibility in the marketplace it needs to succeed.

A good way to determine the potential market for your business is to conduct market surveys. Even if they are as informal as speaking to your friends in your dormitory, fraternity or sorority, surveys get input on whether people would use your business and what variations might make it better. This is a great way to get suggestions and feedback on ways you can enhance your business. Do not get frustrated by possible criticism but rather use it to make your business better. People will always think you should be doing things a little bit differently. To succeed, you will need to determine which pieces of advice will be useful in taking your business to the next level. Always keep your ears open.

It is also good to conduct research of similar business ventures to see how they conduct their business. Understand their strengths and weaknesses. Learn from what other businesses are doing, and take their most effective strategies to incorporate into your own. There is a lot to be learned from studying the way other businesses operate and what has made them successful. Companies such as Proctor & Gamble, Nike, and Microsoft have all remained leaders in their respective industries because of their ability to adapt to new market trends and respond in constructive ways to keep their businesses profitable. Understanding the role your business will play within the market will be crucial.

Another way to jump-start your company is to form partnerships or alliances with other businesses. Make a list of businesses that appeal to a group of people similar to those who would be interested in your product or service. Create a plan that will allow both businesses to benefit from forming a partnership. As you will probably be the smaller of the two businesses, you must be able to offer the other company something it would not normally have access to. Whether you have special contacts within the fraternity and sorority community or friends on athletic teams who can help to spread the word about their business, use all of your unique resources to benefit the partnership. Partnerships give credibility to your business and are a great way to get the word out about your company.

➥ What is the opportunity available in the marketplace?
➥ How do you plan to capitalize on this opportunity?
➥ What research have you conducted to make sure that another company is not already doing this?
➥ Why aren't other businesses doing this?
➥ What potential partnerships would add value to your business idea?
➥ What resources do you have that could benefit a partnership?

Start-up Requirements

Starting your business will require a variety of things, such as product inventory, supplies, extra phone lines, ads or fliers, employees, office space or storage space, a bank account, and perhaps legal advice.

When you start a business, you are forced to compensate for certain deficiencies. This forces you to be creative and to maximize every resource that is available to you. Take advantage of using your school computers and printers, consulting with your business and law professors, talking to your friends for advice, getting friends to help out, speaking with local business owners, and networking with parents of friends who have expertise in your line of business. Entrepreneurs use their resources in the most creative manner to get the most for their business.

➡ What will it take to get your business started?

➡ What resources do you have available to you at college?

➡ What additional resources will be necessary?

Management Responsibilities

There are millions of good business ideas out there; however, it is the implementation of these ideas that matters. How you manage your business will be instrumental in creating a solid foundation from which your company can grow. By being organized and maintaining consistent methods for your business operations, you will be able to promote and track the growth of your business.

If you have hired other people to work with you, you can gain their commitment by treating them as part of the team instead of hired help. Give them a reason to care about the future success of your business. Whether it comes in the form of a cut of each sale or free pizza every week, give them a chance to share in your business success.

Starting a business requires a commitment to the product or service you are providing. Your business will be judged by the quality of this product or service. Take pride in your business and what you are offering the consumer. Make your business a win-win situation in which both the consumer and your business are profiting from the product or service you provide.

Managing your own business will give you excellent experience for your future careers. Employers will be impressed that you have had the chance to manage a group of individuals and took the initiative to start something on your own. You will be steps ahead by gaining this invaluable management experience at such a young age.

➡ Will you be getting any other individuals to work for your business?

➥ How will you be able to keep these individuals focused while not seeming too bossy?

➥ How can you elicit the best work out of the people working with you?

Defining the Business Opportunity

It is essential to clearly define the parameters of your business and what currently exists in the field. When starting a new venture, you must know what you are expecting to get out of your business. Keep in mind that everyone is hoping to make lots of money. Recognize that it is easier to make money in certain fields than others. Also, if a market is already saturated with a variety of businesses, it may not make sense to open another one unless your comparative advantage is significant. Specify exactly what you expect to gain from your business and what you are willing to put in personally before you commit any money to it.

➥ What is the opportunity?

➥ What are you hoping to get out of it?

➥ How can you capitalize on the opportunity?

Finding Obstacles and Ways around Them

It is important to understand the threats and obstacles pertaining to your business. Find out what barriers are prohibiting other people from entering this sort of business. First, write down all of the potential problems you foresee. Whether they are financial or time oriented, list every problem that may arise, then brainstorm ways to solve these problems. Every problem has a solution, so it is up to you to use your creativity to find it. Potential ways around these barriers may include having a proprietary product that you invented, special contacts with a community of potential customers, or even partnerships that solidify your position in the marketplace. You must create a niche for your business and have a comparative advantage that will allow your company to survive and prosper.

➥ What are the barriers to entry?

➥ Why haven't others done what you are planning to do?

➥ What gives your business an edge over competitors?

Strengths and Weaknesses of the Proposed Business

Inevitably, there are going to be strengths and weaknesses of your new business. It is important to maximize your strengths and make up for your weaknesses in a way that will not be exploited by your competitors.

Your strengths will be what give you a comparative advantage over your competitors and allow you to capitalize on the marketplace. Your weaknesses may involve insufficient start-up capital, less experienced personnel, or limited store hours. Fear not; there is no weakness that cannot be overcome with brainstorming and creativity. Some of the most ingenious techniques in business have been discovered because owners were forced to compensate for deficiencies. Use this as a chance to enhance the unique aspects of your business and distinguish it from your competitors.

Remember that most of your competitors will not be college students. Use your own inside knowledge of the college scene and talk to your friends to find out their thoughts on the matter. Your parents and family friends also may have valuable recommendations and resources that could help in starting your business. Use all of your strengths individually and in your surroundings to give your business an edge. Using your creative insight can make your business different and more attractive to your target market.

➡ What are the strengths of your business?
➡ What are the weaknesses of your business?
➡ How do you plan to overcome your weaknesses?

Comparative Advantage

Every new venture must have some form of a comparative advantage to succeed. Your comparative advantage will be what makes your business stand out from the competition. Whether you are marketing your product with a different image to your target audience or you have come up with a new service that is not being offered, identify what is going to be the catalyst in making your business a success. All successful companies have an identity or image they market to their customers in order to attract business. Decide on an image for your business that can give it a comparative advantage your customers can identify with.

➡ What is your comparative advantage?

➡ How will you capitalize on your comparative advantage?

➡ How will you protect your comparative advantage?

➡ What is the image of your business?

The Business Plan

Once you have done the preliminary background work described in this chapter, you can begin thinking about a business plan. One of the most important aspects to starting a business is developing your idea into a business plan. The chapter on business plans later in this book will take you step-by-step through creating your business plan. For now, just organize your thoughts and write down the different aspects of your business and how you plan to develop them. This will help you be better able to understand the elements of your business and how they must all come together for your business to succeed.

Main Points

The entrepreneurial process for each individual is different. Nevertheless, each entrepreneur uses his or her own insight and talents to capitalize on opportunities that others do not recognize or lack the ambition to pursue. Consider these points as you embark upon your entrepreneurial path.

- Opportunities exist everywhere in the marketplace.
- Entrepreneurs see opportunities where others see problems.
- Take advantage of the resources that exist on your college campus.
- Managing a business requires knowing your strengths and your weaknesses.
- Asking questions and listening to others are how you learn and grow as an entrepreneur.
- Setting goals is an excellent way to continuously challenge yourself, your business, and all of the business team members.

Outline your personal entrepreneurial process with the goals and timeline worksheets at the end of this chapter.

Interview

College Entrepreneur Sabeer Bhatia

Owner of Hotmail Corporation, interviewed by the author, October 18, 1998

Q: Tell me a little about your business.

A: Hotmail is the largest provider of electronic mail in the world today with 22 million subscribers growing at the rate of 100,000 new subscribers a day. Its source of revenue comes from advertising and selling products and services to this growing base of consumers. Hotmail is able to accurately target advertising based on a user-provided profile to this base of consumers. At the time of its launch on July 4, 1996, Hotmail was a revolutionary concept because it was the first to make e-mail available on the browser, thus making it globally retrievable. Our subscribers can get access to their e-mail from any Web-enabled computer or device in the world. It has capitalized on its vision to become a leader in this space.

Q: How did you get interested in starting your own business?

A: Sometime in 1995 I got deeply interested in the Internet. I could clearly see that this new medium would cause a paradigm shift in technology and would fundamentally change the lives of people all over the world. At that time I started dabbling with a couple of business ideas I had. One of them was to develop personal databases on the Internet. I recruited Jack Smith, my partner, and this ultimately grew to become Hotmail.

Q: What do you feel is the most challenging aspect of starting and owning your own business?

A: The most challenging aspect, especially in the high-tech business, is getting talented people for specific jobs. The value of high-tech businesses is the accumulation of intellectual capital and the ability to create new products from groups of such talented individuals. In line with this is the challenge to have them work together towards a common goal.

Q: What do you find is the most rewarding aspect?

A: The most rewarding aspect of starting and running your own business is the satisfaction of being your own boss. The uncertainty of survival, the new challenges that an entrepreneur faces each day, and the long hours spent in creating something new are experiences that a successful entrepreneur will carry with them for the rest of their life.

Q: Where do you see the future of your business going?

A: Hotmail is on its way to becoming the dominant platform for Web-based communications. Hotmail has approached this market with e-mail, which is the dominant tool for communications on the Web. It will expand this offering to incorporate new technologies such as instant messaging to create a global communications network.

Q: How do you plan to grow your business?

A: The four steps to growing this business are:

1. Increasing traffic to the Hotmail Web site through aggressive public relations and advertising and by leveraging the strength of the Microsoft network;
2. Converting this traffic to membership by offering subscribers an e-mail account and a handle for instant messaging;
3. Converting a member with a user ID into a loyal user by offering them products and services that enhance the relationship with the user; and
4. Tapping into this strong customer relationship to transact e-commerce on the Web site.

Q: What interests you about what you are doing?

A: The challenge of facing new obstacles every day, the autonomy to make decisions, and the satisfaction of creating a company that has a global impact on society through its 22 million individuals in 230 countries of the world.

Q: What resources were helpful to you when starting your business?

A: Venture capital, the talented work force of Silicon Valley, the availability of high performance machines, and the availability of Internet-related infrastructure to start and operate a Web-based business.

Q: How have you used your business to open other doors for yourself?

A: I have established a name and reputation for myself both in the Silicon Valley and internationally. So far I have not made use of this as I still run Hotmail.

Q: What advice would you give college students starting their own business?

A: Write a business plan. Evaluate the opportunity, size the market, and estimate the requirements for making it successful. Then just do it.

Q: What are your general thoughts on entrepreneurship?

A: Entrepreneurs are risk takers. They are usually individuals who break out of a mold set by society, defy traditional structure, and question the way things are done to create new opportunities for themselves, for their investors, and for the people they employ. One thought that every individual should take away from my success is that the greatest risk in life is not to take a risk at all.

Goals

	Month 1	Month 6	Year 1	Year 2	Year 5
Company					
Financial					
Strategic					
Other					

	Month 1	Month 6	Year 1	Year 2	Year 5
Personal					
Financial					
Strategic					
Other					

Notes

Timeline

Tasks   **Completed By**

Brainstorm   _____

Research and plan   _____

Develop business plan   _____

Assemble the business team   _____

Get financial and legal analysis   _____

Begin product or service process   _____

Schedule marketing and advertising   _____

Open business   _____

Additional:

_____   _____

_____   _____

_____   _____

_____   _____

_____   _____

_____   _____

Notes _____

_____

_____

_____

_____

_____

_____

_____

_____

_____

_____

_____

_____

_____

_____

_____

_____

_____

_____

Part II

The Collegiate Venture Startup

The Business Idea

The Business Plan

The Marketing Plan

Employee Management and Operations

Chapter 3

The Business Idea

Your own business can open many doors and may even develop into a lifetime career.

Mehul P. Vora
Founder of Multimedia Xperts/Internet Media Services

New Ideas

Coming up with new ideas is an exciting part of being an entrepreneur. There is no set way to generate business ideas; however, there are certain ways to extract them. The best way to develop new ideas is to constantly put yourself in new situations and mingle with different types of people. There are endless business opportunities available to those who are discerning enough to recognize voids in the marketplace.

Start by using your personal experiences and expertise to focus on an industry that you are knowledgeable about. Even if you have spent most of your time as a student, you can think about what is not being done on your college campus that students could really use. It is easiest to start a business in an area in which you have experience, but you do not have to limit yourself. Research new industries that you are unfamiliar with so you can determine if your product or service would be successful. Do not be intimidated by an industry you know little about. By investigating different industries, you will learn a lot, even if it does not make sense for you to pursue that particular venture.

For some people, business ideas come easily to them while others need to sit down, focus, and write their thoughts on a piece of paper. Whatever your technique may be, it is always a good idea to write your ideas down with a list of the key elements necessary for your business to succeed.

Brainstorming

Brainstorming is an exciting way to generate new business ideas. It stimulates your creative side to come up with potential ideas.

Make your brainstorming sessions very relaxed and informal. It is important when brainstorming to write down absolutely everything that comes to mind and in no specific order. You will have plenty of time to go back later and arrange your thoughts into a formal structure.

A good way to start is to first write down your interests. Next, list your talents and areas of expertise. Then list contacts and resources you have that will give you a competitive edge in the marketplace. Think about experiences you have had with a product or service that could have been done better. When you have all of these down on paper, start drawing lines between areas where there may be a match and list all the business ideas that come to mind, no matter how trivial. Once you have a list of ideas, you can continue brainstorming and go into more depth.

Brainstorming is an essential part of developing your idea. Even once you have started your business, continue to brainstorm. This will help you come up with new ideas to incorporate into your business, ways to improve your product or service, or possibly even ideas for future businesses. An integral part of being an entrepreneur is thinking of new ways to capitalize on opportunities in the marketplace. Your brain should be continuously busy thinking of how to make your business more successful.

Believe it or not, ideas are the easy part of starting a business. The execution of an idea into an actual business is what will determine the success of your company. This is why researching the industry and writing a business plan are so essential. Thorough research gives you the background knowledge, and a business plan gives you a game plan for getting your business going and determining what it will take to succeed.

➡ What industries do you have experience with or you are interested in learning about?

➡ What is it that interests you about this type of business?

➡ What other opportunities could be done in this line of business?

➡ What products or services are not available on your college campus?

➡ Is there something being done at other universities that is a huge success and is not being done at yours?

Industry Research

Once you have selected your idea and done the preliminary brainstorming, it is time to take your idea to the next level, which is to research the industry. Researching your idea is a very important step for your business. You want to make sure that you do not spend weeks trying to start a business when there is a competitor doing the same thing and offering a better price down the street or on the Web. It will also help you to understand the financial requirements of the business. Some businesses cost a lot less to start than others.

The first thing to do is to find out if anyone is already doing something similar to what you have in mind. You can conduct this research by performing searches on the World Wide Web using, for example, Yahoo Business, Hoover's Online, or the Lexis-Nexis database at your school library.

Talk with friends at other schools to see what exists at their college and if they would be interested in a business like yours at their university. Search the World Wide Web to find relevant information that relates to your new business. E-mail other business owners in different parts of the country who are not in direct competition with you to see how they run their business and if they have any tips for you. Thoroughly researching business ideas is an important key to making you a successful entrepreneur.

Your next course of action is to research your future competitors. Do not jump into anything without thoroughly understanding the competition and how you are going to differentiate your business from theirs. Go to their place of business and investigate how they run their operation. If possible, become a customer or even an employee to get an insider's understanding of their product or service and how they manage their business.

You can use your campus library to research possible competitors in the marketplace through such programs as Lexis-Nexis and Dun & Bradstreet. Lexis-Nexis is a database that allows you to search for specific information on business news and companies. Dun & Bradstreet can be used for detailed information on millions of companies all over the world. Analysts spend all of their time covering specific industries; therefore, it makes sense to find out their thoughts regarding the market you are about to enter. Also, search the Internet for other companies that may be doing something similar in different parts of the nation.

Lastly, analyze how your competitors operate. Whatever your idea may be, when you study other businesses that are doing something similar, you can capitalize on what they do well and learn from their mistakes. Thorough research will help you to identify and develop the comparative advantage of your business over competitors and determine the steps necessary to make it a success.

Check out ways that existing campus businesses market their product or service to college students. Investigate working in partnership with the university, the school newspaper, campus clubs, or even campus sports teams. In this way you can determine what successful methods you are going to borrow from these existing businesses and what will give your business an advantage in the marketplace.

The end result of conducting research is that you have in-depth information on what types of businesses already exist in the marketplace so that you can strategize how your company will be more successful.

➥ What tools and programs have you used to research your idea?
➥ What industry contacts have you spoken to about your idea?
➥ Who are your existing future competitors?
➥ What are the marketplace trends?
➥ What will be your company focus?
➥ How is your business different from others that currently exist?

Evaluation Techniques

Once you have decided the type of business you want to start, it is important to test your idea to make final additions and adjustments. An idea is really a prototype that does not actually become a business until it passes a series of tests and receives final approval. Do not be frustrated if, after you have tested your idea and gotten feedback, you decide to not go any further. Entrepreneurial thinking will help you come up with many ideas, most of which will not become thriving businesses. The key is to develop a way to test your ideas to see if they would be profitable in the marketplace.

This is a good time to bounce your idea off of friends, relatives, or any other people who may have knowledge of the industry you are considering entering. Get their advice on what they think of your business idea and how it can be improved. Speak with as many different types of people as you can to get various perspectives on how you can improve your idea. Realize that people are always quick to point out flaws in your business idea, so do not be put off by this. The important part is to maintain the belief in your idea while you incorporate their good ideas into your existing framework.

Being at college, you are surrounded by available resources that can give you feedback on your business idea. Your fellow students and your professors may have valuable insight into starting a business. Get your classmates to take surveys to find out what to include in your business and ways in which you can fine tune your product or service. Speak with a law professor to determine the steps you need to take to obtain licenses or to incorporate your business. Speak with a marketing professor to get ideas on how you can advertise your business to the college community and beyond. Try to understand how local businesses succeed in luring college students to their stores.

Some colleges are even developing programs that help students with business ideas. Do not be afraid to contact a university representative to see what they think of your idea. The end result may be some good advice, a partner, or even a customer. The more people who become involved by giving you constructive feedback, the more successful your product or service will be.

If your business focuses on the needs of college students, make sure to get their insight on what might improve your business. Big companies are often very out of touch with the college environment. By being a college student, you are in tune with the college scene and have the best sense of what sort of product or service will excel in this type of marketplace. When evaluating your idea, it is important to focus on the comparative advantage of your business and whether it is truly different from that of your competitors.

As nice as it is to get compliments on your business, constructive feedback will be more useful in perfecting your idea. Do not become frustrated with the criticism you receive from various people. Just remember that each individual has a different set of preferences that alter their perceptions. By speaking with a diverse group of people about your idea, you are more likely to get feedback that will help customize your product or service to the largest group of people possible.

➥ What do your family and friends think of your idea?

➥ What professors can you speak with to fine tune your idea?

➥ Does your college have an entrepreneurial department?

➥ What constructive criticism can you implement to provide a better product or service?

Big Dream Approach

There is nothing wrong with having dreams to become some day the next Bill Gates or Donald Trump. Having goals and aspirations is what it takes to start out as an entrepreneur. Then having the confidence, desire, and persistence to do whatever it takes to succeed is what will keep you in business.

Although you will probably be forced to start on a small scale with your new venture, do not let this discourage you. Dell Computers was started in a college dormitory room, and Nantucket Nectars was started as a summer job between semesters. All entrepreneurs have to start somewhere, and having dreams and goals is the only way to visualize making it big time. Even if your idea is only intended to be small scale, the lessons learned from starting your own business will be valuable for the rest of your life. Entrepreneurial thinking will teach you to capitalize on opportunities in the marketplace as well as in life. Dreams only become reality if you go for it.

Main Points

Entrepreneurs come up with many different types of business ideas. The implementation of the idea is what turns it into a successful venture. Consider the following points when evaluating and implementing your idea.

- Before you begin doing any work on your business idea, make sure to conduct extensive research to understand what already exists in the marketplace.
- Incorporate the strengths of your competitors into your business and learn from their mistakes.
- Create a comparative advantage for your business that potential customers can readily identify with and benefit from.
- Because new ideas are the lifeblood of your business, continually look for new opportunities and encourage your business team members to do the same.
- Always believe in yourself and your idea.

Explore potential business ideas with the worksheets on brainstorming, research, resources, and competition at the end of this chapter.

Interview

College Entrepreneur Mehul P. Vora
Original owner of MultiMedia Xperts/Internet Media Services, interviewed by the author, October 15, 1998

Q: Tell me about your background.
A: I am an Asian-American. My parents immigrated to this country during my formative years. The majority of my schooling occurred on the West Coast. I attended Franklin Middle School and Franklin High School, both offshoots of the original Franklin Academy in Maryland. Continuing in the footsteps of one of my role models, Ben Franklin, I attended the institution founded by him, the University of Pennsylvania. My tenure there involved the pursuit of dual degrees in finance and computer science engineering. Due to diverse interests, my curriculum also included several foreign languages and varied liberal arts courses.

Q: Tell me a little bit about your business.

A: Our firm began operations under the name MultiMedia Xperts. At a later date, this was changed to Internet Media Services. Our primary function was to offer full-service Web consulting for businesses interested in using the World Wide Web as a marketing medium to reach consumers or other businesses. We began as a hypertext markup language (HTML) authoring shop for the Web and developed into a Web solutions company, providing hosting, authoring, promotion, and maintenance for interactive, attractive, and commerce-enabled Web sites. Some ancillary services also included general information technology consulting.

Q: How did you get interested in starting your own business?

A: A close colleague shared with me the strategic vision that Internet and Web consulting would skyrocket with the advent of the free browser and the proliferation of the personal computer. In 1993 and 1994, both of us witnessed the release and dominance of the Mosaic and Netscape Navigator browsers. We jumped on the opportunity to publish personal Web pages through our free school servers utilizing the newest version of HTML. As our experience and knowledge blossomed, other students, professors, and friends began tapping us for help and advice. Additionally, both of us received positive feedback from our internship employers in the summer of 1995 concerning the initial concept of starting a consulting business. We recognized an emerging demand and decided to capitalize on it after careful evaluation and strategy formation.

Q: Is this something you always planned on doing?

A: Without a doubt, yes! Gauging market characteristics and capitalizing on supply and demand inequalities or niche opportunities was always the strategy. My partner and I had several other business plans in various stages of completion; however, this one was most attractive. Entrepreneurship runs in our veins.

Q: Had you ever started a business before?

A: As a young adult, I got my feet wet in several different ventures but never at the operating or management level.

Q: What do you feel is the most challenging aspect of starting and owning your own business?

A: The most challenging and often most overlooked requirement for the successful operation of your own business is discipline. Discipline to work horrendous hours, to know when to call it quits, to maintain focus through rough as well as prosperous times, and above all else, discipline in maintaining sanity.

Q: What do you find is the most rewarding aspect?

A: Without a doubt, there are no managers who are functionally capable of running every business detail. However, by running your own business, you get exposure, albeit at a limited level, to almost all aspects of the company, financial, operating, accounting, human resources, marketing, et cetera. Thus, having a thorough understanding of the fundamental impact of every piece of the company puzzle enables you to be a better manager. I find this the most rewarding and the most useful. Of course, making lots of money is fun, too.

Q: Where do you see the future of your business going?

A: We have sold all rights to our trade name. This was not the initial exit strategy but has served such a purpose. The transition to Internet Media Services was simply a way to continue maintenance of our current clients. We are not pursuing any further operations.

Q: How do you plan to grow your business?

A: There are no growth plans at this point. During the start-up phase, we researched the most viable marketing channels and examined several joint venture opportunities with traditional publishing, advertising, and marketing agencies. Our strategy to build the business was to team with these firms, allowing both of us to offer a broader and relatively complete array of services to our clients.

Q: What interests you about what you are doing?

A: My mind is highly technical and detail oriented. Web authoring, site development, and other aspects of Web consulting require immense attention to detail. At the same time, these activities allow creativity and imagination to pervade color schemes and motifs. In other words, this line of work exercises all parts of the brain. Additionally, being an owner as well as a consultant offers the highest level of flexibility and complete discretion with the selection of clients.

Q: What resources were helpful to you when starting your business?

A: The Wharton School of Business where we were students had an extremely helpful Small Business Development Center. Another resource derived from our business and entrepreneurship class professors. Our mainstay, however, was the Web itself. We used other Web sites to enhance our technical knowledge, keep up-to-date with Internet and Web standards, and monitor the competition.

Q: How have you used your business to open other doors for yourself?

A: The whole experience of starting my own business has leveraged my résumé beyond belief and serves as a central talking point in interviews. Also, the experience helped me gain entrance into seniors-only entrepreneurship classes while I was still a junior.

Q: What advice would you give college students on starting their own business?

A: Starting your own business requires a serious time commitment, varying slightly with the type of business. Students must either possess or be willing to quickly learn essential time-management skills. This means more than just owning and using a planner. Time management involves the prioritization of time requirements, demands, and needs. The most often heard reason for failure among college entrepreneurs is losing focus on classes and grades and, to a lesser but more severe degree, the inability to complete the curriculum and obtain their degree.

　Your own business can open many doors and may even develop into a lifelong career. However, nothing can replace a college degree, regardless of the education received there. That's right; the simple paper on which your degree is printed adds immense value. Most entrepreneurs will confirm that work experience greatly outweighs classroom theory. Nonetheless, the first door into corporate America is still guarded by the need to have a piece of paper that confirms the receipt of a collegiate-level degree.

Q: What do you feel can be learned from starting a business in college?

A: Whether through success or failure, collegiate entrepreneurs will surely learn many of the soft skills upon which most of today's reputed business schools seem to focus. Some of these skills include negotiation, conflict resolution, and mass communication. Another critical skill obtained from starting a business in college is the ability to plan on a strategic level. Consequently, the ability to execute that business plan often becomes a great skill for the well educated and experienced collegiate entrepreneurs.

Q: What are your general thoughts on entrepreneurship?

A: Entrepreneurship is not for everyone. Clearly, some people cannot function in an environment in which so much responsibility is placed directly on their shoulders. Others are distressed rather than energized by having to write their own checks and meal tickets. Careful thought, planning, and consultation must occur before venturing into the ranks of true entrepreneurs.

With that disclaimer, I highly encourage college students to go into business for themselves. This country affords immense opportunity to the bright, educated, and honest businessperson. Working through the appropriate channels and always maintaining a high level of ethics will be its own reward. Finding a market niche or arbitrage opportunity makes for a bonus.

Brainstorming

Talents

_____
_____
_____
_____
_____

Interests

_____
_____
_____
_____
_____

Experience

_____
_____
_____
_____
_____

Special resources available

_____
_____
_____
_____
_____

Research

Competitors

_____
_____
_____
_____

Strengths and weaknesses of competitors

_____
_____
_____
_____

Potential partnerships

_____
_____
_____
_____

Marketplace trends

_____
_____
_____
_____

Barriers to entry

_____
_____
_____
_____

Comparative advantage of your business

_____
_____
_____
_____

Notes _____
_____
_____
_____

Resources for Business Ideas

Professors

_____
_____
_____
_____

Friends

_____
_____
_____
_____

Small Business Developments Centers

_____
_____
_____
_____

Small Business Administration

_____
_____
_____
_____

Local business owners

_____
_____
_____
_____

Alumni

_____
_____
_____
_____

Campus groups

_____
_____
_____
_____

Notes

_____
_____
_____
_____
_____
_____
_____
_____
_____
_____
_____
_____
_____
_____
_____

Comparison to the Competition

The Competition

Competitor #1 _____

Years in business _____

Market share _____

Price strategy _____

Product or service _____

_____

Strengths _____

_____

_____

Weaknesses _____

_____

_____

Competitor #2 _____

Years in business _____

Market share _____

Price strategy _____

Product or service _____

_____

Strengths _____

_____

_____

Weaknesses _____

_____

_____

Competitor #3 _____

Years in business _____

Market share _____

Price strategy _____

Product or service _____

_____

Strengths _____

_____

_____

Weaknesses _____

_____

_____

Your Strengths and Weaknesses

Strengths _____

_____

_____

_____

_____

Weaknesses _____

_____

_____

_____

_____

Strengths _____

_____

_____

_____

_____

Weaknesses _____

_____

_____

_____

_____

Strengths _____

_____

_____

_____

_____

Weaknesses _____

_____

_____

_____

_____

Chapter 4

The Business Plan

Make sure that you have some clear idea of where you are headed before you make any decisive moves towards implementing your ideas.

Guatam Godhwani
Founder of AtWeb

Writing a Business Plan

Writing a business plan is a very important step in starting a business. Even in the early stages, it is important to organize your ideas in a business-plan format. Doing this will help you develop and expand your ideas. Writing a business plan forces you to analyze your idea in every way possible to create a well-thought-out plan for your business to succeed.

Putting all your ideas down on paper can stimulate new ideas for your business; however, the idea is the easy part of a business. Implementing the idea is the hardest part because it is what will determine the success of your business. That is why the business plan is so crucial.

A business plan is like a blueprint, a program of action for implementing the different components of your business. While each business is different, there are certain aspects that are the same.

- You must have the financial resources to start your business,
- Your business must have a comparative advantage over your competitors,
- You must be able to reach your target market and inform them of your product or service, and
- You must be able to effectively manage your business.

Writing a business plan forces you to think through and explain your thoughts in each of these areas and more.

The business plan is the document that potential investors, partners, and advisors will want to see. It will describe your business and help them understand your vision for the success of your business. The business plan is also meant to entice the reader to want to become a part of your business.

Whether preparing a business plan to show potential investors, your friends, your parents, or anyone else, the presentation of the document itself is critical. Using the proper format and highlighting the key points will make a lasting impression on the reader. The business plan should be a creative and professional presentation of your idea, including financial statements and research to support your conclusions.

Most people who write business plans do not take the time to learn how to prepare them in the proper fashion and often present the financial statements, for example, in a format that is difficult for the reader to understand. They also fall into the trap of projecting unrealistic goals because they have not done their homework and are not aware of competing businesses in their industry. This chapter will help you write a business plan that expands on your ideas, gives the reader an enticing look at your exciting business opportunity, and presents financial projections in a standard format, all of which will impress even experienced investors.

Turning your idea into a business is a full-time endeavor, and developing your business plan is the single most important step you can take toward that goal. Especially in maximizing your potential to receive capital, it is vital that you create a business plan that will not only guide your company but also allow outsiders to picture where you are going and how you plan to get there. (Pierce 1998)

➡ What experience do you have with writing business plans?

➡ Who can you approach for guidance, comments, and evaluation?

Components of a Business Plan

In this chapter, you can follow a business plan from start to completion. After describing what each section of your business plan should include, there will be an example given from the corresponding business plan of Speedy Room Cleaning. This was an actual service business started by two individuals who discovered an opportunity in the college marketplace. Realizing that college students hate to clean and that most cleaning services cater to the higher-income market, they saw an opportunity that was not being taken advantage of. Going to school in Boston, they were surrounded by many college campuses that presented an immediate target market for their service.

The 12 components of a business plan are:

- Cover
- Introductory page
- Table of contents
- Executive summary
- Industry focus
- Description of venture
- Merchandising and operations plan
- Marketing plan
- Organizational structure
- Assessment of risk
- Financial plan
- Appendix

Cover, Introductory Page, and Table of Contents

The cover of your business plan should have your business name, logo, and a brief caption or slogan for your business. It should be in color and should grab the attention of the reader. Getting the attention of the reader is very important because opinions can be formed in the first few pages. Get some of your creative friends to help you with the name and graphic design for your business. The more people you include, the more resources you will eventually have available to your business. Employ the special skills of your friends and find a way to get them involved.

The introductory page should include the names of the owners, a three- to four-sentence description of your business, and the amount of money you are seeking, if any, to start your business. The introductory page is simply meant to introduce the reader to your idea and to arouse their curiosity and interest.

It is a good idea to put a statement at the bottom of this page protecting your business idea. Although you will probably not have someone trying to steal your idea, it is best to protect yourself.

The table of contents should clearly outline the contents of your business plan. Make sure to include the basic sections of executive summary, industry focus, description of venture, the merchandising or operational plan, marketing plan, organizational structure, assessment of risk, and financial plan.

Make sure your business name does not infringe on any other businesses. You can determine this by doing a search on the Web, through reference books in libraries, or even in your area's telephone book business pages if yours is a local service-type business. It is not necessary to hire lawyers to perform such a search. It is usually large companies that hire people to make sure no new companies are infringing on their rights to their trade name. In fact, they are required to do so in order to keep those proprietary rights. Use your creativity and common sense to come up with an original business name.

➡ What is the name and slogan of your business?

➡ Have you developed a logo?

➡ In a sentence or two, how would you describe the business opportunity?

Sample Introductory Page

Co-owners: Mark Jacobs and Rachel Pollock

Description of Business: Speedy Room Cleaning will offer affordable rates to help college students keep their living units clean. Speedy Room Cleaning will take care of everything necessary to clean a student's dorm room, fraternity or sorority house, or off-campus apartment. Services include washing dishes, doing laundry, vacuuming, removing trash, mopping, sanitizing, and organizing.

Slogan: Run by students for students

Financing: Speedy Room Cleaning will need approximately $10,000 for initial inventory, advertising, and employees' wages.

This report is confidential and is the property of the owners listed above. It is intended for use only by the person to whom it is transmitted, and reproduction or divulgence of any of its contents without the prior written consent of the company is prohibited.

Executive Summary

The executive summary serves as a snapshot of the entire contents of your business plan. The executive summary should range from one to three pages in length and include the main highlights from your business plan. It is usually written after you have completed the contents of the business plan so that it can be a synopsis for the reader of what is in the document. Oftentimes people will read only this section to decide if they are interested in reading any further. The executive summary is, therefore, the most important section of your business plan. While it can seem difficult to encapsulate your entire business idea in one to three pages, this is your chance to create a succinct, informative summary that will spark the reader's interest and set the tone for the remainder of the document.

➥ What is the opportunity that exists in the marketplace?

➥ What will your business offer its customers?

➥ Why are other companies not doing this?

➡ What is your comparative advantage in the marketplace?

➡ What supplies or human resources will you need to start your business?

➡ What financing will be necessary to get your business up and running?

Sample Executive Summary

College students are notorious for living in messy rooms. Many never have the time or inclination to take care of their living quarters nor the finances to hire traditional cleaning services.

Speedy Room Cleaning plans to perform various tasks to help college students keep their dorm rooms, fraternity houses, and apartments clean. This will be done by offering affordable rates for dishwashing, laundry, vacuuming, removing trash, mopping, sanitizing, and general organizing.

The amounts charged, $10 to $40 per unit, are more affordable for college students, especially when several students share the cost. By offering an affordable service that will attend to all of their cleaning needs, Speedy Room Cleaning anticipates an incredible opportunity to create a large clientele.

Students will be able to schedule a cleaning via e-mail, phone, or our Web site. Initial projections for Speedy Room Cleaning are to service approximately five to ten rooms a week while building the customer base to 40 to 50 jobs a week. After paying part-time employees, ourselves, and certain overhead expenditures, Speedy Room Cleaning anticipates making a minimum of approximately $5 profit per job. This will result in an estimated profit of $1,125 a month. Pending possible partnerships and expansion to other nearby universities, this amount may be greatly increased in a short period of time.

Speedy Room Cleaning plans to employ other university students and local individuals for cleaning. In addition to being part-time employees, they will have active roles in the development of our business. Being run by students for students, Speedy Room Cleaning already has a potential clientele who will be interested in our service immediately. In addition to word-of-mouth advertising, we also plan to post fliers on campus and develop a referral commission structure for employees and friends who bring other clients into our customer base.

We also plan to use the Internet to work with students nationwide to create their own branches of Speedy Room Cleaning. We plan on expanding our scope of business once we have created the proper inroads at other colleges in this region and then nationwide. By providing college students with the incredible experience of running a business and having university sponsorship, Speedy Room Cleaning plans to eventually create a nationwide network of branches.

Speedy Room Cleaning expects to create a profitable niche for itself while providing a quality service that will benefit the lives of college students nationwide.

Industry Focus

The industry focus section of your business plan gives the reader an understanding of the general landscape of the industry you will be entering. You should analyze the industry and the current trends that are affecting the marketplace. Here is where you report what industry experts are saying about current trends from the information you found in Hoover's, Dun & Bradstreet, or any of the brokerage research reports offered online. It should also describe both the niche your business is going to focus on and who your competitors are. Anything that you can use to verify the information you present to the reader will help validate your idea.

➥ What industry will you be entering?
➥ What do industry insiders say about current market trends?
➥ Who are your competitors?

Sample Industry focus

Speedy Room Cleaning will enter the cleaning services industry, a market that has several major competitors. Currently the main industry service provider is Molly Maid, followed next by independent house cleaning businesses that also occupy this segment of the market. To date, these groups have made no attempt to break into the college marketplace. Some universities offer laundry services, but these are often slow and inefficient due to off-site locations.

Speedy Room Cleaning will capitalize on personal relationships with the student body as well as university officials to bypass barriers to entry for this potential market. Establishing these relationships at an early stage will enable us to build our own network of loyal customers and supporters. In addition, Speedy Room Cleaning plans to expand to other nearby universities and eventually other campuses nationwide. We will use our special formula for personal relationships and the slogan of "Run by students for students" to give us an advantage over competitors.

By being the first company in this region to develop a successful formula that capitalizes on the students' personal relationships with friends and university officials, Speedy Room Cleaning will be able to create a niche in the industry in a way that will minimize future competition.

Speedy Room Cleaning will also tailor its services in a way that fits the needs of college students. Cleaning agencies generally do not have low-priced options and will only do entire cleanings of a unit. These high prices prevent college students from using their services. Speedy Room Cleaning plans to offer more flexibility as well as more affordable individual rates and group rates for fraternity and sorority houses and apartments. We will also offer one-time monthly, semester, and year-long price-discount packages to our customers.

Speedy Room Cleaning plans to market our services under headings that college students can identify with. The Quickie is a 20-minute cleaning that involves sweeping, mopping, vacuuming, dusting, removing trash, and picking up and folding clothes. The Mid Term is a service that involves all of the above in addition to bathroom cleaning. The Final Exam includes all of the above in addition to kitchen clean up and is intended for an entire apartment or fraternity or sorority house. Laundry can be added to each of the services for an additional fee. There will be variations of the above so that each college student can customize our services to fit his or her needs.

The comparative advantage of Speedy Room Cleaning is the way in which we are able to offer affordable rates and flexibility to college students and to market our services in a manner they can more easily relate to and benefit from. By employing college students, we will be able to understand first hand what it will take to satisfy our clientele. These students will also have an active voice in the management and future of Speedy Room Cleaning; thus we can make this a learning experience for the students, even giving them the opportunity to open new branches across the country.

No college student enjoys cleaning or doing laundry, but there has been no alternative in the past. By offering an easy, affordable, and friendly service that will take care of everything for them, Speedy Room Cleaning will truly be a success.

Description of Venture

The description of venture section is a detailed explanation of your business. It should give the reader an in-depth understanding of the opportunity and how you plan to implement your business. Because each reader will have a different level of understanding, you should explain your venture in the simplest terms possible. People are usually not interested in ideas they do not understand.

It is a good idea to give some examples of businesses that are in your industry and how your company will be different, particularly if you are looking for investors.

- ➡ What product or service is your business providing?
- ➡ What is the comparative advantage of your business?
- ➡ What competitors are there in the marketplace?
- ➡ What resources will you need for your business?
- ➡ How will your business make money?

Sample Description of Venture

Speedy Room Cleaning will be a service that cleans college students' rooms in dorms, apartments, and fraternity and sorority houses. Speedy Room Cleaning will offer a variety of services that will appeal to the needs, preferences, and financial situation of our college student customers. Speedy Room Cleaning will offer an affordable alternative for cleaning that has not been available before.

Most college students are only familiar with cleaning services if their parents have used them. These traditional cleaning services do not cater to college students because they do not see them as a profitable segment of the marketplace. Their high fixed costs and overhead do not allow them to lower their rates enough to make the prices attractive to college students.

Speedy Room Cleaning will be run by students who have friends on campus and contacts with university officials and professors. These contacts will create an immediate customer base and will help spread positive word-of-mouth advertising. With our unique marketing efforts and affordable rates of $10 to $40 dollars per unit, students will be inclined to use a service that makes their lives a lot easier.

Speedy Room Cleaning will create an employee bonus system for referrals that team members and other individuals bring in. Depending on the type and length of the job, they will be rewarded with a commission of approximately 10 percent of the total price of the job. Giving student employees a financial reason to get their friends to use our service will help to increase sales and augment marketing efforts. Speedy Room Cleaning will offer these incentives to every employee.

Speedy Room Cleaning will also work with the university to offer some of its positions as work-study jobs. The university employs the majority of students who work on campus in some sort of work-study program, usually with cafeterias and libraries. By creating a program with the administration in which students can work for Speedy Room Cleaning as part of the work-study program, it will create a ready supply of employees for our business. We will present this plan to the university with the idea that students who take part in Speedy Room Cleaning will get entrepreneurial experience through first-hand exposure to running a small business.

The first endeavor for Speedy Room Cleaning will be started at Boston College and be managed by two senior students. Speedy Room Cleaning will initially hire approximately five students on a part-time basis and will hire additional students as demand increases after the first few months of operation.

Speedy Room Cleaning plans to expand to nearby universities and then to college campuses nationwide. As expansion occurs, Speedy Room Cleaning will hire a key person at each university to run that particular operation. Speedy Room Cleaning will collect royalties on every sale at these other locations in exchange for an operating manual, guidance on our formula for success, and support programs for each new business.

Having professors help us prepare the contents of the business plan and financial statements will also assist us in getting further contacts within the university administration. Creating a formula for success by employing students and developing key relationships with university officials will be the major factors in establishing successful operations on college campuses across the country. Competitors will then have extreme difficulty entering the marketplace due to our strong ties with administration officials and our pipeline of student employees.

Having spoken with both university officials and professors, we are confident that our services will be a hit in the marketplace.

Merchandising and Operations Plan

This section of your business plan explains how you intend to sell your product or deliver your service. As stated earlier, having the idea for a business is the easy part. The implementation of the idea is what will determine the success of your venture. Here is where you describe that implementation.

Once you have carefully designed an efficient plan to produce your product or deliver your service, you will have more time for other areas of business development. Be sure to take advantage of the helpful resources you have available to you on your college campus. Whether you post fliers on kiosks throughout campus or speak with professors in the business department, your college campus has many resources for you as an entrepreneur.

If you plan to produce a product, you will need to outline the process and what requisites will be necessary for its creation. You will also need to decide whether you will be working out of your living space, in a spare room in a campus building, or in some other location. By writing down every step required to produce your product, you and the reader will have a clearer vision of the business.

If you are developing an entirely original invention or product, you may even want to think about obtaining a patent for it. Chapter 8 covers whether a patent is necessary and the application process.

If your business is providing a service to the marketplace, you will need to outline how you will provide it and what requisites you will need. If you are starting a service business, you will probably be able to work out of your living space to begin with. Running a service-oriented business requires paying extremely close attention to detail, carefully organizing your resources, and assuring top-quality customer service.

➡ What steps are involved in bringing your product or service to the marketplace?

➡ What friends, family, or professors can you consult for advice in this area?

Sample Merchandising and Operations Plan

Speedy Room Cleaning plans to hire five employees to help in the early stages of our business at our first location. Once an order is placed, the job is staffed with employees who are available on that date. Based on the type of order, each employee will have a specific job to do in the living space. This will help to expedite the cleaning process and maximize the productivity of our employees. Each employee will be paid $7 an hour plus commissions for each job performed, as well as a quarterly bonus that will be awarded based on the revenue generated by the company as a whole for that month.

Speedy Room Cleaning will purchase supplies, costing approximately $300, from cleaning product companies as well as bulk food stores that sell cleaning materials in large quantities. To minimize costs, Speedy Room Cleaning will purchase less expensive second-hand cleaning equipment such as vacuums for approximately $450. Based on the demand on campus, Speedy Room Cleaning plans to stock enough equipment and supplies to staff two jobs simultaneously. As demand grows, we will increase our inventory of cleaning supplies and equipment.

Employees will first be given a course in cleaning techniques and then be guided by group leaders during jobs. Upon completion of each job, the group leader will fill out an evaluation form to highlight areas that need improvement in the future. The customer will also be given an evaluation form to fill out at his or her convenience for submitting suggestions on how to perform better in the future. Speedy Room Cleaning feels very strongly about adopting the suggestions of customers into the operational plan. Customers' and employees' ideas for new services or modifications of existing ones will be used to improve performance.

Speedy Room Cleaning will purchase liability insurance, costing approximately $35 a month. This is necessary in the event of an accident on customer premises. While the chances of this are slim, Speedy Room Cleaning wishes to protect itself from any possible liability.

The operating procedures for Speedy Room Cleaning are based on providing top-notch service to our customers in the most efficient manner possible. We will rely on the customers to be the tuning fork to perfecting the cleaning services offered. Speedy Room Cleaning will obtain evaluation comments from customers immediately after a cleaning is finished and later by mailing questionnaires that offer a 10 percent discount off of their next cleaning if completed.

Speedy Room Cleaning plans to set up the operations in the most efficient way in order to build a solid foundation for profit and growth.

Marketing Plan

The marketing section of your business plan should include the image you wish to create for your company and how you plan to reach your target market. Chapter 5 goes into detail on the different ways to reach potential customers. However, this section of your business plan should at least outline the methods you are going to employ.

Companies such as McDonald's, Coca Cola, Federal Express, and others have been extremely successful because they have effectively created a name brand. Even though their businesses started out as small companies, they eventually grew as a result of hard work, ambition, and luck. Creating a successful brand is all about building the right image for your business. When creating an image for your business, make sure that it clearly conveys a particular message that your customers can identify with.

Effectively promoting your business through the right media, at the right time, and for the right cost will help improve your efficiency in reaching your target audience. The marketing section should describe what methods you are going to use to reach your target audience. There are a plethora of different media available to use in your marketing campaign. You want to choose the ones that are the most cost effective while reaching the most people in your target market. This section of your business plan should explain your reasoning for choosing these methods.

➡ What is the image of the business you are building?

➡ What advertising methods are you going to use?

➡ What resources are available to you on campus that will enhance your marketing plan?

Sample Marketing Plan

Speedy Room Cleaning's image will be one the students can easily understand and readily identify with, that of inexpensive, fast, and reliable cleaning that frees up their time for doing other things. Our goal is an image that helps students realize how much easier it is for us to clean their rooms than for them to do it themselves.

Speedy Room Cleaning plans to concentrate most of our marketing efforts in creating a buzz on college campuses about our service. Our four most cost-effective marketing options are a referral bonus system for individuals who bring in new business, partnerships created with the university, fliers posted on campus, and word-of-mouth advertising by students.

Further marketing efforts will include advertising in campus newspapers, banners on collegiate Web sites, and listings in college job classifieds.

Speedy Room Cleaning plans to increase advertising efforts at particular times of the year when peak use is expected, such as just prior to parents' weekend, graduation, homecoming, and other special weekends on campus. Speedy Room Cleaning has chosen these advertising methods as being the most cost-effective means of reaching the greatest number of students.

Organizational Structure

This section of the business plan should describe how you plan to structure your business. The foundation of every business are the people who work for it. This section should describe the talents and experience that each person brings to the business. Even if this is your first business in an area that you have not had any previous experience with, list other attributes and talents that will show your desire to succeed and your track record for success.

The most important resource your business has is a strong staff. If there are other individuals such as industry contacts, professors, or friends who will be assisting you in your endeavors, it is a good idea to list them and their qualifications. This will show the network of resources that your business is developing.

It is also a good idea to form an advisory board for your business. This can include professors or other individuals who have expertise in the industry in which you are starting a business. They can serve as an excellent resource and as a guide for your business.

Every person who is affiliated with your business should be described in the business plan. Include an organizational structure chart to illustrate the hierarchy of your personnel, even if it is just you and another person.

Taking the time now to set up the infrastructure of your business will help you better manage your business as it grows.

- ➡ What individuals are going to be a part of your business?
- ➡ What personality traits are you looking for in individuals interested in joining your business?
- ➡ What professionals would be a valuable addition to your advisory board?

Sample Organizational Structure

Each cleaning group will have a team leader who organizes the work to be done and addresses all questions and concerns from the customer. The team leaders will report directly to one of the two managers who will oversee the operations of the company. The other manager will oversee marketing and new business development.

Speedy Room Cleaning will hire individuals who are interested in entrepreneurship and have had prior experience in a start-up business. We also intend to form additional relationships with business professors and university officials for their personal recommendations on exemplary candidates who have an entrepreneurial flare and may want to get involved with the business. Employees will then be encouraged to get others involved as well as provide their own insight on how the company can grow. As the business grows, we will hire additional students to work in all areas of the business. Each individual who is part of our business will have a vested interest in the success of the company. Quarterly bonuses will be given to each employee with special incentives for personal achievement. The goal is for every employee to feel like a valued member of our business.

Speedy Room Cleaning will strive to create an organizational structure that promotes teamwork and lays the foundation for future expansion.

Co-owners: Mark Jacobs and Rachel Pollock
Staff: Jennifer Goldberg, Richard Anderson, Bryce Cooper, Brian Andres
Advisory Board: Dr. Ellen Richardson, Marc Hashet, Dillon Lauden

This is the first official business venture for Mark Jacobs and Rachel Pollock. They have both worked independently for other start-up ventures in the services industry. Joining Mark and Rachel are Jennifer, Richard, Bryce, and Brian, all of whom have experience in the cleaning industry. Two of these individuals are students and two are local community members who previously worked for a large corporate cleaning company. Speedy Room Cleaning is fortunate to have these professionals on our advisory board: Dr. Ellen Richardson, chair of entrepreneurial studies at Boston College; Marc Hashet, professor of marketing at Boston College; and Dillon Lauden, a local community business leader.

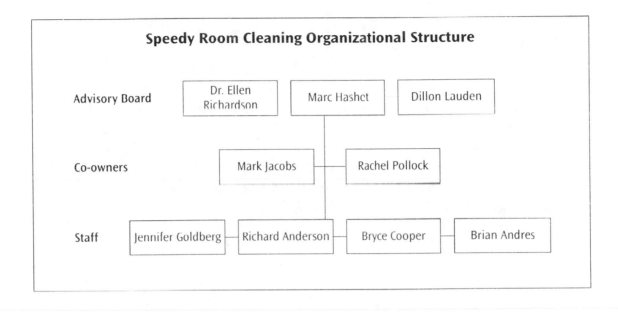

Assessment of Risk

Every business plan needs a section that explains the risks associated with starting the business. It is unrealistic to think that your business has no risks and that it is a sure thing. Market conditions, timing, liability issues, and potential competitors all play an important role in determining the level of risk associated with starting a business. Entrepreneurs who are able to see these risks before they affect their business are able to capitalize on their foresight.

After listing the potential risks related to your business, explain your strategy for dealing effectively with these issues. Here is where you can show that you are the kind of entrepreneur who is a forward thinker who tries to foresee problems in the future. Learning to be a forward thinker and deal with problems that may not even come about for another month, year, or decade, if ever, is an important skill that is learned from starting your own business.

- ➡ What current risks are there associated with starting your business?
- ➡ What marketplace trends could affect the industry and become future risks?
- ➡ What competitors will play an important role in the success of your business?
- ➡ How will you deal with each of the current and anticipated risks?

Sample Assessment of Risk

College students have long been known for having unkempt living quarters, and this trend shows no signs of letting up.

Two risks associated with Speedy Room Cleaning entail the offering of a service to college students that has never been offered before and creating a synergy between the local community, university, and the student body. To overcome these risks, Speedy Room Cleaning will strive to create a comfortable and complementary atmosphere for all three of these groups. To integrate ourselves with the local community, university community, and student body, the company will get involved with campus and other local activities to become well known and ensure a good reception to our business.

A third risk is that another cleaning business could begin to focus on students as a target market. We are confident that by offering low prices, having students on the business team, and projecting an image of a professional company that particularly understands the needs of college students, our business will establish a presence and grow steadily.

A fourth potential risk is that other college students would start up a cleaning business competing with ours. We believe that this is unlikely because of the capital required to start such a venture and the network of individuals necessary to run it successfully.

Once Speedy Room Cleaning has established itself in Boston, expansion to other schools will further solidify our position because it will allow entrepreneurs at other universities to get involved by starting their own branch, instead of starting an entirely new business on their own.

Financial Plan

The financial section of the business plan is intended to give the reader a snapshot of the start-up costs, balance sheet, income statement, and cash flow of your business. Do not worry if you have not had any experience preparing financial statements. They may seem more intimidating than they are. Once you understand the standard format, you will be able to vary it to fit your business. Chapter 7 in this book and the worksheets at the end of that chapter will help you create financial statements for your business.

Because your business has probably not begun making money, the financial statements will be projections of anticipated costs and earnings. It is important to make realistic projections and assumptions when preparing your financial statements. In addition, include a justification for each of the assumptions you make regarding the projections for your business, even if it is just a statement at the bottom of one of the pages.

Taking the time now to prepare these statements correctly will help in recording the earnings of your business later. Once you have created a format for your financial statements, you will be able to plug in the monthly numbers to determine the profitability of your business. By presenting the financial section of your business plan in a clear and generally accepted format, most readers will be able to understand the numbers and make a judgment on the potential of your business.

➡ How much money will it take for you to start your business?

➡ Have you itemized all of the costs associated with running your business on a monthly basis?

➡ What are the different potential levels of sales that you anticipate to generate?

➡ Are there any individuals who will be investing in your business?

Sample Financial Plan

Speedy Room Cleaning plans on using $3,000 in start-up funds to purchase cleaning supplies, begin a marketing campaign, and pay part-time employees until revenue begins coming in. The expensive items such as vacuum cleaners shall be one-time capital expenditures for the business. The other items such as cleaning solutions, laundry detergent, mops, sponges, and other supplies will be purchased on a recurring basis.

The following documents display the projected start-up costs, balance sheet, income statement, break-even analysis, and statement of cash flows for Speedy Room Cleaning. These projected statements represent comparable numbers for the cleaning services industry.

Employees are paid $7 an hour plus commissions of 10 percent of a job and bonuses on a quarterly basis depending on the overall success of the company. Speedy Room Cleaning will also be purchasing help-wanted ads and marketing advertisements.

Due to the range of services we offer, projected revenue will accrue from fees charged of $10 to $40 per room. For dwelling units with multiple rooms, such as fraternity and sorority houses, the fee will be approximately 2 to 3 times the above numbers. The revenue numbers show conservative estimates to account for slow times during the year.

Speedy Room Cleaning Projected Start-up Costs

Vacuum cleaners	$ 450
Cleaning supplies	300
Legal fees	287
Marketing materials	300
First-month salaries	263
	$1,600

Speedy Room Cleaning
Projected Balance Sheet
End of First Year

Assets

Current assets

Cash	$7,200
Accounts receivable	350
Supplies	50
Total current assets	7,600

Fixed assets

Equipment	652
Less depreciation	0
Total assets	**$8,252**

Liabilities and Owners' Equity

Current liabilities

Accounts payable	$ 200
Other	100
Total current liabilities	300

Long-term liabilities

Notes payable	0
Long-term liabilities	150
Total liabilities	450

Owners' equity

Rachel Pollock	800
Mark Jacobs	200
Investor	900
Retained earnings	5,902
Total owners' equity	7,802
Total liabilities and owners' equity	$8,252

Assumptions

Numbers are based on assumptions in income statement from revenue B numbers.

Only difference from income statement is that balance sheet reflects bonuses paid out of 50% of earnings from the year.

Speedy Room Cleaning
Projected Income Statement

	Jan	Feb	Mar	Apr	May	June	Jul	Aug	Sept	Oct	Nov	Dec
Revenue A	875	875	875	875	875	875	875	875	875	875	875	875
Revenue B	1,650	1,650	1,650	1,650	1,650	1,650	1,650	1,650	1,650	1,650	1,650	1,650
Start-up costs	1,600	0	0	0	0	0	0	0	0	0	0	0
Marketing	250	250	250	250	250	250	250	250	250	250	250	250
Salaries	263	263	263	263	263	263	263	263	263	263	263	263
Telephone	20	20	20	20	20	20	20	20	20	20	20	20
	2,133	533	533	533	533	533	533	533	533	533	533	533
Income A	−1,258	342	342	342	342	342	342	342	342	342	342	342
Income A to date	−1,258	−916	−574	−232	110	452	794	1,136	1,478	1,820	2,162	2,504
Income B	−483	1,117	1,117	1,117	1,117	1,117	1,117	1,117	1,117	1,117	1,117	1,117
Income B to date	−483	634	1,751	2,868	3,985	5,102	6,219	7,336	8,453	9,570	10,687	11,804

Assumptions

Revenue A is based on a staff of 5 individuals and 35 cleanings a week at $25 a cleaning.
Revenue B is based on a staff of 5 individuals and 55 cleanings a week at $30 a cleaning.
Staff are paid the equivalent of $7 an hour plus bonuses on income on an annual basis.
Cleanings are based on 30-minute intervals.

Speedy Room Cleaning
Projected Break-even Analysis for First Year

	Jan	Feb	Mar	Apr	May	June	Jul	Aug	Sept	Oct	Nov	Dec
Revenue	690	690	690	690	690	690	690	690	690	690	690	690
Start-up costs	1,600	0	0	0	0	0	0	0	0	0	0	0
Marketing	250	250	250	250	250	250	250	250	250	250	250	250
Salaries	263	263	263	263	263	263	263	263	263	263	263	263
Telephone	20	20	20	20	20	20	20	20	20	20	20	20
Income	-1,443	157	157	157	157	157	157	157	157	157	157	157
Income to date	-1,443	-1,286	-1,129	-972	-815	-658	-501	-344	-187	-30	127	284

Assumptions

Revenue is based on a staff of 5 individuals and 23 cleanings a month at $30 a cleaning.

Staff are paid the equivalent of $7 an hour plus bonuses on an annual basis.

Salaries do not include bonuses, which are distributed on a quarterly basis and are not reflected here.

Speedy Room Cleaning
Projected Statement of Cash Flows

	Jan	Feb	Mar	Apr	May	June	Jul	Aug	Sept	Oct	Nov	Dec
Revenue A	875	875	875	875	875	875	875	875	875	875	875	875
Revenue B	1,650	1,650	1,650	1,650	1,650	1,650	1,650	1,650	1,650	1,650	1,650	1,650
Monthly expenses	2,133	533	533	533	533	533	533	533	533	533	533	533
Revenue A cash flow per month	–1,258	342	342	342	342	342	342	342	342	342	342	342
Revenue A cash flow year to date	–1,258	–916	–574	–232	110	452	794	1,136	1,478	1,820	2,162	2,504
Revenue B cash flow per month	–483	1,117	1,117	1,117	1,117	1,117	1,117	1,117	1,117	1,117	1,117	1,117
Revenue B cash flow year to date	–483	634	1,751	2,868	3,985	5,102	6,219	7,336	8,453	9,570	10,687	11,804

Assumptions are the same as those specified for the income statement.

Appendix

The appendix includes any additional information that does not fit specifically in the business plan. This is a good place for industry reports, résumés of key personnel, and any additional information that will give the reader a clearer idea of your business. Some readers will never look at the appendix while others will scrutinize every page. Not every business plan has an appendix. If you do include one, make sure it has only pertinent information that will provide additional validation of your business concept.

Sample Appendix – Résumés of Key Executives

Marc Jacobs

Education

Boston College, candidate for Bachelor of Arts Degree in 2000

Business classes taken: accounting, marketing, finance, entrepreneurial management. Grade point average: 3.75

Experience

JAAM Lawn Care Services, summer 1999

Started business with four partners providing lawn care services to the local Boston market. Involved in all aspects of operations, marketing, and finances. Was part of team that increased revenues to $35,000 for the three-month period.

Benshaw and Lokem, Attorneys at Law, summer 1998

Interned at Boston law firm for the summer. Involved in contract preparation, proofreading, and other office duties. Worked with senior lawyers and was allowed to sit in on certain meetings.

Activities

Treasurer, Delta Tau Delta. Responsible for all aspects of managing $100,000 annual budget and making financial projections for the upcoming year.

Tennis Team. Varsity tennis team player for all three years of college. Practiced for approximately three hours a day, six days a week for the entire school year.

Sample Appendix – Résumés of Key Executives

Rachel Pollock

Education

Boston College, candidate for Bachelor of Science Degree in 2000

Business classes taken: management, entrepreneurial studies, public relations, marketing

Grade point average: 4.00

Experience

JAAM Lawn Care Services, summer 1999

Started business with four partners providing lawn care services to the local Boston market. Involved in all aspects of operations, marketing, and finances. Was part of team that increased revenues to $35,000 for the three-month period.

Turner Broadcasting Network, spring 1999

Interned with television network in its marketing and public relations department. Involved with analyzing new advertising media and creating new slogans for nationwide advertising campaign.

Activities

Alpha Chi Omega

Active member of Alpha Chi Omega sorority for previous three years of college, participating in all social and rush activities.

The Green Lantern Honor Society

Member of honor society for students with grade point average of 3.95 and above.

Main Points

Creating a business plan is a necessary step that requires you to organize your thoughts and develop your ideas. It should give your readers a clear vision of what the business is about in a concise, standard, and easy to understand format. Consider these points when writing your business plan.

- The business plan should be a marketable document that informs and excites the reader and makes him or her want to become involved.
- Prepare the financial statements in a generally accepted accounting format and do not get fancy.
- Investors often look more closely at the quality of the business team members, even more so than the business idea itself.
- Enhance your business plan with colorful, glossy inserts and by binding it upon completion.

Take great care in preparing your plan; it is the road map that will lead you to where you want to go. (Pierce 1998) Begin formulating your plan with the business plan worksheet at the end of this chapter.

Interview

College Entrepreneur Guatam Godhwani
Owner of AtWeb, interviewed by the author, October 20, 1998

Q: Tell me about your background.
A: I grew up between India, Texas, and California. I finally settled in California and attended the University of California at Berkeley to study computer science and business administration.

Q: Tell me a little bit about your business.
A: AtWeb provides tools to objectively measure and consistently improve Web sites.

Q: How did you get interested in starting your own business?
A: Peter Weck, a classmate at Berkeley, and I were working together at the time and decided we would take a couple of days off to check out Internet World, the premier Internet trade show, while it was in the area. Peter asked his roommate, Thomas Knudsen, another Berkeley classmate, to join us, and I

also asked my brother, Anil Godhwani, to join us. We were all so excited about the opportunities available in Internet space that within several weeks we had started AtWeb.

Q: What do you feel is the most challenging aspect of starting and owning your own business?

A: I think the most difficult aspect was translating this lofty vision into something attainable. It took us a long time to figure out what steps needed to be taken to actually implement our ideas.

Q: What do you find is the most rewarding aspect?

A: Every time I see one of our products, whether it's on the Internet or someone is mentioning it in the press or just in walking around the office, it reminds me that all of this came from a vision that the other founders and I had at Internet World one day. And to see it grow to such a point is something that is very fulfilling.

Q: Where do you see the future of your business going?

A: With the endless possibilities on the Internet, I really see AtWeb providing all the services necessary for a Web site, with the exception of creation. In just six months, we have tripled our staff and currently expect growth to continue at the same rate.

Q: How do you plan to grow your business?

A: We are introducing several new product lines in the next few months that build on the foundation we have already established, that of Web-site maintenance and promotion. Our new product lines will address Web communication and measurement.

Q: What interests you about what you are doing?

A: I really feel passionate about the Web and its capabilities. Similarly, with the amount of energy our staff has, we can barely keep up with our own ideas. Pairing the enthusiasm of AtWeb with the Web leaves infinite possibilities.

Q: What resources were helpful to you when starting your business?

A: The most helpful resource we found was the chairman of our board of directors, Jerry Crawley, and other Silicon Valley veterans who have really helped us shape our business and grow without the typical pains associated with such growth.

Q: How have you used your business to open other doors for yourself?

A: I think it has given me a lot of insight and introductions I would not have had otherwise.

Q: What advice would you give a college student interested in starting his or her own business?

A: Make sure that you have some clear idea of where you are headed before you make any decisive moves towards implementing your ideas. Each step you have already allotted for will save you a lot of time in the future.

Q: What are your general thoughts on entrepreneurship?

A: I have yet to find anything as fulfilling as walking into the office in the morning and knowing that we are all working towards the same ideals. While it is time consuming and difficult at times, it is rewarding in the end.

Business Plan Preparation

Cover Page

Name of business

Logo

Slogan

Telephone number, mailing address, e-mail and Web-site addresses

Introduction

Name of owner(s)

Brief statement of business

Amounts of financing desired, if any

Confidentiality statement

Table of Contents

Each section listed with its page number

Appendix or supporting information

Executive Summary

Brief description of your business, to include these areas:

• The industry

• Your comparative advantage

• Financing

• Key members of the business team

• Any other important information

Industry Focus

Industry information

Market trends

Competitors

Barriers to entry

Future of the industry

Description of Venture

Detailed description of business

Your product or service

The target market

Location of business

Competition

Business team members

Summary

Merchandising and Operational Plan

Production process or service delivery

Comparison to major competitors

Requisites needed

Marketing Plan

Strategic image

Methods of advertising

Advertising budget

Implementation and analysis plan

Organizational Structure

Management

Personnel

Advisory board

Organizational chart

Assessment of Risk

Risks

Competitors

Barriers to entry

Future developments

Methods to deal with risks

Financial Plan

Overview

Sources and uses of funding

Capital equipment

Assumptions

Start-up costs

Break-even analysis

Projected income sheet

Projected balance sheet

Projected cash flow statements

Appendix

Résumés of key personnel

Marketing materials

Competitor information

Industry reports

Letters of encouragement

Chapter 5

The Marketing Plan

Once you have the goal you want to achieve in mind, a good entrepreneur will discover ways to get there.

Michael C. Mathews
Founder of JAMM Enterprises

Exposure

Having a great business idea is only part of what it takes to build a successful business. You can have the greatest product or service in the world, but if no one knows about it, your business will not succeed. It is important when constructing your business to decide how you are going to reach your target market.

There are several different ways to get the word out about your business. You can advertise directly to potential customers by posting or handing out fliers, placing ads in the school newspaper, creating a Web site, or writing press releases. More indirect methods include forming partnerships with local businesses or even teaming up with the college itself. Your advertising strategy should incorporate all of these methods to the greatest extent possible.

The Target Market

When starting a new business, you must decide upon the group of people to whom you are marketing. It is important to include as broad a market as possible to avoid alienating any group of people or limiting your sales potential. You then must customize your product or service to fit the specific needs of the group of people you have targeted.

While in most cases you want to market your product or service to the largest possible group of people, you can also succeed selling to a very narrow target group, especially if your business fits a partic-ular niche in the market. Vegetarians, handicapped people, minorities, or athletic teams, for example, can be very profitable to specialize in. Potential target markets can also include college students, children, music lovers, video lovers, and many others. Also keep in mind that a lot of the money available on college campuses is from parents. If possible, find a way to market your product or service to the parents of students. Allow them to purchase items directly or have them for-warded to their children in the form of gifts, rewards, or just-thinking-of-you items.

It is usually best to avoid a target market that you are not familiar with. If you do not truly understand their needs, it can be your downfall in the long run.

An important factor to consider is the financial situation of the people you are selling to. You can have a truly wonderful product or service, but if your targeted group does not have the money to pay for it, your business will fail. On the other hand, if they do have the money, you may be able to make your idea more upscale. Always design your business to fit the needs, desires, and financial situation of the people you are targeting.

➡ Who is your target market?
➡ How can you attract other customers?
➡ Are you overlooking any potential groups?

Marketing Finances

Virtually every business requires money to start but not necessarily a lot of money to be successful. Some of the most successful compa-nies in the world have been started in college, which is a time in most people's lives when they are not flush with cash. Do not be discouraged by the fact that you may not have the capital to start your business, let alone build a marketing campaign. If you are creative enough, there will be a way for you to succeed.

For example, a student conceived the idea for Federal Express in an entrepreneurial class at the Wharton School of Business at the University of Pennsylvania. The student received only a B grade on the idea, yet he began the business and has developed his creative concept into an industry giant. He may not have had the money to start the business full time in college, but he held onto the idea and began it later when he did. Others, such as Stephan Paternot and Todd Krizelman of theglobe.com, pooled the money they had together with help from their parents and then landed a $20 million investment a couple of years after they graduated, most of which went towards marketing and building the brand name.

When budgeting, try to get the most bang out of every marketing dollar. Do not be discouraged by a lack of readily available funds for marketing; just use your creativity to overcome any financial hurdles.

➡ What will your marketing costs be?

➡ How much revenue do you expect to generate from marketing?

Marketing and Advertising Strategies

The following marketing strategies are just some of the many options available for a business. Although not all will be perfectly suited for your business, you can employ the ones that will yield the greatest results for the fewest dollars.

➡ How do you plan to get the word out about your business?

➡ What are the specific goals for your marketing campaign?

Word-of-mouth Advertising

Word-of-mouth advertising is the best and least expensive form of advertising. The highest compliment another individual can give your business is to recommend it to another person. This immediately lends credibility to your business and is absolutely free. All you have to do is make sure you keep your customers very happy and look for ways to improve your product or service. Remember that this can also have the reverse effect, however, if you do not provide a quality product or service. The more people saying positive things about your business, the better.

Friends

Friends represent an excellent source of marketing for your business because word-of-mouth marketing is the best endorsement for any business. This will be an advantage that you will have over all of your competitors, especially if your business is targeted at college students. By actually being part of the student body, you have the inside scoop on the college marketplace as well as classmates and friends who will talk about your business.

Do not forget about your friends at other colleges across the nation. They can be a valuable tool in getting feedback on your idea or helping to bring in business from another school. Investigate whether they have anything like your business on their campus and how that product is marketed. Have them ask a few of their unbiased friends to see what they think of your proposed product or service.

A great way to involve friends at other colleges is to reward their customer referrals by giving them a portion of every sale that comes from their school. You can even make them the official representative for their university, thus truly making them feel a part of the business team. This will help you reach more customers with minimal expense.

If you run a service business, establish a relationship in which you provide them all the guidance to set up another branch of your business at their school. Offer them the opportunity to get their friends involved and give them a percentage of what they sell. By forming a network of representatives across the country, you will expand your business without having to be there physically. This will help to generate new sales that would have never been possible otherwise.

Referrals

Referrals are one of the biggest sources of revenue for businesses of all sizes. Having employees and satisfied customers talk about your business will often create a buzz that will help increase sales for a fraction of traditional advertising costs. You can even approach other more established businesses in your field and ask them to refer their overflow customers to you.

➡ How will you create a buzz about your business around campus?

➡ What friends can help you spread the word about your business?

➡ What friends do you have at other colleges?

Campus Connections

If your business caters to college students in some manner, try to incorporate numerous campus-related events and campus groups into your business. This is an excellent way for your business to gain credibility and establish a presence on the college campus. A good way to get involved and develop these connections is to sponsor different campus events or offer discounts to certain campus groups.

Campus Events

There are campus events happening daily at colleges nationwide. Whether it is a faculty party, a sports event, parents' weekend, or a campus holiday, there are ways to capitalize on these activities. These can include special marketing efforts or offering some sort of special promotion.

Think about ways to market your product or service in a way that appeals to the attendees at these events. A savvy entrepreneur will always capitalize on special events and opportunities that will help the business grow and generate more revenue.

➡ What campus events could correlate with your business product or service?

➡ What people do you know who participate in these events?

➡ What would be the best way to market your business to the people at these events?

Campus Groups

Among sports teams, acting groups, debate teams, music groups, language clubs, community service groups, and honor societies, there exists a wide range of student groups on college campuses. Consider how to market your product or service to them in a way that makes it worthwhile for them to do business with you. Speak to your friends in campus groups and on athletic teams to find out their ideas on the best way to market your business.

Fraternities and sororities also represent a distinct portion of the population on many college campuses. Activities such as Greek week, sorority and fraternity parties and formals, and rush represent possible opportunities for your business. Attempt to incorporate a marketing plan that effectively targets these organizations. Speak with your friends in different fraternities and sororities about how to become involved in winning their business. Whether making T-shirts for parties, creating party favors, renting tuxedos for formals, or organizing the catering for rush events, fraternities and sororities represent very active social groups who require the services of a variety of different businesses.

There are endless opportunities to market to such campus groups. If you work to create a close relationship with these groups and gain their trust, the result can be a beneficial arrangement for both sides.

- ➡ What resources on campus are available to help promote your business?
- ➡ Which of your friends will be able to promote your business through their clubs, groups, or athletic teams?
- ➡ What products or services do these groups use?
- ➡ How could you attract their business?

Print Media

Print media include fliers, newspaper and magazine advertisements, direct mail pieces, press releases, and any other information relayed to prospective customers in print format. The major advantages of print media are that you can convey a specific message and that you can focus on specific promotional events or holidays. Depending on the type of print media you use, you can even target your advertisement to a specific group of people. For example, fliers posted around campus are most likely to attract the attention of college students while an ad in the local paper in the business section is likely to attract an entirely different type of person. Be aware that there are many different price levels of print media. Fliers are probably the least expensive whereas newspaper ads can cost hundreds of dollars, depending on the size, frequency, and location of the ad.

Fliers

One of the most cost-effective and successful ways to reach college students is by posting fliers on kiosks and other display areas throughout the campus. Create an eye-catching design or have your advertisement printed on colored paper to attract the attention of individuals walking by. Grab their attention with large, bold words such as *money* and *free*, two words college students are very familiar with.

You can even design your own fliers as well as brochures and ads on your computer with a publishing program such as Microsoft Publisher. Make sure to include your phone number and Web address where people can learn more about your product or service. Post your fliers on kiosks and other display areas throughout campus, in university buildings, and in local businesses to help get the word out. Posting fliers is especially effective on college campuses because of the high amount of foot traffic in a small, concentrated area.

➡ Where are there places to post fliers?

➡ How can you draw attention to your fliers?

Advertisements

The school newspaper is read by virtually every student, faculty member, university employee, and a considerable number of parents. This can be an especially effective way to get the word out about your business. Although an ad in the newspaper can be expensive, it is one of the best ways to reach the greatest number of people associated with your college. Ads can cost anywhere from $5 for a few lines in the classified section to $300 for a half-page display ad with color. However, many schools offer discounts if you are a student. Also, there are often lower rates for those who advertise on a regular basis.

Consider the timing of your ad. You may want to wait until there is a significant event or special weekend on campus that correlates with the product or service you are providing to maximize your advertising dollars.

➡ When is the best time to place your advertisement?

➡ What will it take for your business to cover the cost of the ad?

Press Releases

Another way to get the word out is through press releases. Press releases are a good way to gain some free publicity for your business. Write up an announcement about your business to send to the campus and local newspapers, magazines, and TV and radio stations. The best times to issue a press release are when you start your business, offer a new product or service, bring on new employees, or reach an identifiable and noteworthy business milestone.

Use the worksheet at the end of this chapter to write a press release for the opening of your business. Send it to as many reporting entities in your area as possible. Although some will probably not print your release, those that do will generate free publicity for your business and may even contact you about writing a follow-up news article about your company.

➡ What are the important points to include in your press release?

➡ What local media should you send the press release to?

The Internet

The Internet has turned college into a wired world where you can communicate with your friends at other schools by e-mail. It also provides entrepreneurs with an entirely new way to market and sell products and promote services. Web sites are an excellent and inexpensive form of marketing for your business. It is possible to convey an amazing amount of information about your business and even allow customers to make purchases directly from your Web site. The Internet, and more specifically Web sites, have revolutionized the way business is conducted. Use the detailed Web-site creation section in this book to build a Web site for your business. This can be one of the best tools for marketing your business.

Partnerships

Partnerships are an excellent way to begin a business because they offer you an established company to learn from and a pre-existing customer base to market to. It can be a real asset to form partnerships with existing businesses in industries that have cross-promotional opportunities. Because a partnership gives your business credibility and exposure to a ready customer base, it is an excellent way to give your business a jump start.

It can be difficult to form these partnerships, however, because your business is new and has not established itself. Therefore, you must give your potential partner something to make it advantageous for them to participate. The key to forming a partnership with another company is to determine exactly what you can provide them to make it worthwhile. One way to appeal to other businesses is to market your valuable network of friends at colleges nationwide. Help them market their product or service so that it will appeal to more college students. Many large corporations have programs that employ college students exactly for this purpose. Or you can give them a cut of every new sale that the partnership generates for your business.

Companies are always looking for cross-promotional opportunities to expand their businesses. Do not be intimidated by the size, scope, or reputation of any company you are interested in partnering with. Just find the right person to speak with and present them with a clear and concise plan that will benefit both of your companies.

The university administration is also an excellent candidate for potential partnership opportunities for your business. Determine how your product or service will improve the lives of the college students and how a partnership with the university would be beneficial for both sides. Speak with your professors to get any contacts and tips on how to present your business idea in a way that will interest them and will gain their support and cooperation.

In teaming up with a larger business, you have to consider just how much you are willing to offer. For example, when Stephan Paternot and Todd Krizelman founded theglobe.com at Cornell University, they desperately needed additional capital to grow their business. Michael Egan, founder of Alamo Rent-A-Car, agreed to invest approximately $20 million dollars in their business; however, they had to give up ownership of nearly 70 percent of the company. Although this may seem like a lot, that capital was what enabled their business to grow. Their company went public on the Nasdaq Stock Exchange in early 1999, ultimately creating more value in the long run.

Forming partnerships and making contacts will create a solid base for your business to springboard from. Partnerships can also provide your business with access to an entirely new group of resources. Use this opportunity to learn from your partner. Start by compiling a list of possible partners and identify the ways in which you can benefit each business.

➥ What businesses could you form a partnership with?

➥ How do your business idea and your resources add value to their business?

➥ Do you or your friends have any industry contacts whom you could talk to about a partnership?

➥ Is there potential to work with your university?

➥ Do your professors know any people or alumni whom you could contact?

Main Points

No matter how good your idea is, your business will not succeed if no one knows about it. Consider these major points when formulating a marketing strategy for your business.

• Define your target market and decide how your business fits in with their needs, desires, and financial situation.

• Word-of-mouth advertising is the best and least expensive form of marketing.

• Consider how a Web site would benefit your business.

• Partnerships are an excellent way to establish credibility for your business and give you a pre-existing customer base.

• The best way to get the word out about your business is to promote it in as many different ways and places as possible.

Begin developing the marketing plan for your business with the marketing strategy overview and press release worksheets at the end of this chapter.

Interview

College Entrepreneur Michael C. Mathews

Owner of JAMM Enterprises, interviewed by the author, June 21, 1998

Q: Tell me a little about your background.

A: In 1998, I graduated from Lehigh University in Bethlehem, Pennsylvania, with a B.A. in accounting. I majored in accounting because I felt it was the best way to learn about every aspect of a company. I started JAMM Enterprises while at college at Lehigh to make a little extra money.

Q: Tell me about your business.

A: JAMM Enterprises was a T-shirt business which targeted the local college, high school, and area athletic teams. I started the business with a good friend of mine. There are at least four to six athletic teams per school, per season, not to mention the different levels, freshman, junior varsity, and varsity. We would talk to team captains and coaches and tell them we could provide them with high quality T-shirts at a low cost which they could help design. The coaches liked the idea of someone from their school making the T-shirts and were very excited to work with us.

Once we had a deal with a team, we took advantage of our school's resources. We used their computers and art supplies during the design phase. During the production phase, we supplied the T shirts but used the school's silk screening equipment, photo equipment, and paint. Our only costs were the price of the T-shirts which we purchased from a local price club, our time and effort designing and producing the T-shirts, and a very small lab fee paid to the art teacher for use of the studio. Distribution wasn't difficult because we would have the team captain or coach come to us to pick up the T-shirts.

Q: How did you get interested in starting your own business?

A: Money. We needed money to pay for our spring break. We would sit around and think about how we could make money and what people need. We started thinking about the people we knew. Our school was very actively involved in athletics, as we were too, so we knew what the teams were like. We just kept brainstorming and then realized how many athletic teams the school had during the year and how many students were involved.

In addition, the most important thing was that we fully understood what the students wanted. They wanted T-shirts for their team which had certain qualities: the school name, reference to their team, cool graphics and design, and an aggressive, cocky saying. Each of us had taken a few art classes and knew about the supplies our school had and how easy it would be to use them. The local businesses that made T-shirts were currently charging way too much for the T-shirts. The idea just took off from there.

Q: Is this something you always planned on doing?

A: Did we sit around for 10 years wanting to start a T-shirt business? No. What we did do, though, was to sit around and continually ask, "What do people need? What would make their lives easier or better? What don't they have now?" These questions were always on our minds. If you spend enough time thinking about something, I mean really thinking and brainstorming, ideas will come. The important thing to remember while you are coming up with ideas is not to put limits on them. Don't start thinking, "Oh, that sounds really expensive," or "That might be too hard," or "Someone already tried that." That stuff doesn't matter because once you have the goal you want to achieve in mind, a good entrepreneur will discover ways to get there.

Q: Had you ever started a business before?

A: No. This was our first one.

Q: What do you feel is the most challenging aspect of starting and owning your own business?

A: I think there are two. One is that thousands of people have ideas, good ideas. However, only a few people act on those ideas. Why doesn't everyone act on their good entrepreneurial ideas? They are scared, scared because it might be too risky, they are not sure if it will work, or they are too comfortable with what they currently have. Starting a business is a risky proposition; there is no doubt about that. But a good entrepreneur knows how to reduce his or her risk and maximize potential. After you do your homework, find out what people want, and know how you are going to give it to them, then it will not be as risky.

Then there is margin. That is the other great challenge. The way of the past was to do cost-based pricing. You knew what you wanted to make, determined how much it would cost to make it, and then charged a certain percentage higher than that cost. Today, the type of market you are in is going to determine how much you are going to sell your product for. This is called price-based costing. You know the price, and once that is set, you find a way to make the product for a certain cost which will give you a certain profit. So once you know the price of the product, if you are a good entrepreneur, you have to work exceptionally hard to determine how you can lower all of your production costs and expenses so that you can enjoy the highest margin possible.

Q: What do you find is the most rewarding aspect?

A: Seeing one of my T-shirts being worn around school. Overhearing someone ask the person who is wearing the T-shirt, "Hey, where did you get that? It's cool. I want one."

Q: How do you plan to grow your business?

A: As I said before, there are so many athletic teams during the school year. We need to start talking to more of them and get their business instead of having them go somewhere else. The key is to start to develop relationships. Most likely you are going to know someone on each team. Start talking to them. Tell them what you are doing and what you have to offer. Have them mention it to their coach to see what they think. Go to some of their games, talk to your friend on the team after the game, let the coach see you, and introduce yourself. After a while, start talking to the coach and tell him what you can do for the team. You will hopefully have a few teams under your belt at this time so he can see your products and feel better about doing business with you because others already have.

Q: What interests you about what you are doing?

A: Having a part in every aspect of the business. You have to wear so many different hats, as a salesman, an analyst, an accountant, an engineer, a marketer, and so on. When this occurs, you can't help but learn more and more about each respective function. The important thing to remember is that you don't have to be an expert in each area; there are already people who are, and you can use them as resources.

Q: Have you used your business to open other doors for yourself?

A: Sure. We got to meet a lot of people we wouldn't have otherwise. Some of the coaches were teachers, also. Once they saw the initiative we were taking, how organized we were, how driven we were, it gave us a lot more to talk about. We developed better relationships with them, and that carried over to when we were in the classroom. We also got exposure to coaches of teams we wanted to be on. If you are on a junior varsity team, hopefully you will be talking to the varsity coach to see if he would like to order T-shirts from you. If you do a good job, he will see what kind of person you are and get to know you better while you are telling him how well you are doing on junior varsity and how you can't wait to make varsity. Also, anything you do on your own will be a huge résumé builder. When people start seeing the initiative and effort you have put forth to start a business or two, they will be much more interested in you for their company.

Q: What do you feel can be learned from starting a business in college?

A: The experience and knowledge you can get from starting your own business is more useful than any class you can take. The skills you develop, such as how to focus, organize, delegate, present, and network, are priceless and are not going to be developed while you are reading a textbook.

Q: What are your general thoughts on entrepreneurship?

A: When some people think of entrepreneurship, they instantly think of failure. I think of endless opportunity. Think about it; Nike, Gateway, Dell, and Federal Express are just some of the companies in which one person had an idea and then acted on it. They knew what their customers were looking for and supplied them with the product they needed at a reasonable price, and as time went on, they have kept getting bigger and better. There is never going to be a time when all the ideas of the world are used up or have been thought of by someone. They are out there. It is up to you to find them and then do something about it.

Marketing Strategy Overview

Target Market

_____

_____

_____

Marketing Strategy

_____

_____

_____

Advertising Budget

_____

_____

_____

Advertising Methods
   Word of mouth
      Friends at your college
      Friends at other colleges
      Customer and employee referrals
   Campus connections
      Campus events
      Campus groups
   Print media
      Fliers
      Advertisements
      Press releases
   The Internet
   Partnerships

Sales Force Members

_____

_____

_____

Notes _____

_____

_____

_____

_____

_____

Press Release

New Business Announcement   **For Immediate Release**

_____
(Date you mail this)

Contact: (Give contact person's name, phone number, fax number, and e-mail address)

_____

_____

_____

_____

(Name of business)
(Your city and state) (Date) –
(Describe your company, its product or service, and its advantages to customers)

_____

_____

_____

_____

(Give pricing and availability)

_____

_____

_____

_____

For more information, contact: (Give business name and how to contact you)

_____

_____

_____

_____

Chapter 6

Employee Management
and Operations

I knew that you could teach entrepreneurship as a process, as long as you see it as a way of leading and a way of managing. It turns out that this is the way that most people see Silicon Valley, not necessarily as a haven of technology but as a way of doing business.

Tom Byers
Professor, Stanford Technology Venture Partners

Managing Your Business

Managing your business is an important skill that will be crucial for success. You will be responsible for every facet of your business and be the final authority on all decisions. Because you assume the most responsibility for your business and are the ultimate decision maker, you are the most rewarded by the financial gains of your company. Seeing your business grow is a very gratifying part of being an entrepreneur and will give you confidence as a leader.

As your business grows, you will have additional responsibilities to fulfill. There comes a time when you need to take the proper steps to ensure you do not grow too quickly. If business gets out of hand, you may not be able to provide the same level of quality because you are inundated with work. As this happens, you may want to hire additional people to work as part of your business team.

Hiring Additional People

Starting a business in college requires a significant amount of time. Not everyone is willing to sacrifice all their time and energy to start a business. Utilizing all available resources and hiring additional personnel will allow you to moderate the amount of time you spend on your business. The important part is that members of your business team share your enthusiasm and commitment to the business.

College campuses are an excellent place to find additional people to help with your business. The career planning and placement office should be able to post a job opening announcement for free. This is a great way to reach the entire student body and to promote your business as well. You can also place a help-wanted advertisement in the school newspaper classified section or list the opening on one of the Web sites devoted to job searches, such as Jobtrack (www.jobtrack.com) and CareerPath (www.careerpath.com).

Potential business team members do not necessarily have to be on your campus. Having business team members at other campuses to sell your product or offer your service opens up a whole new market for your business. Even if you just need some part-time help, students from other schools represent a great pool of potential employees.

You can probably hire your fellow students for anywhere from $7 to $10 an hour plus any other perks you can offer. Most students who get jobs during college need the money, so make sure that you are able to pay them what they deserve.

➡ How much time will you have to commit to your business on a weekly basis?

➡ How many people will you need to hire?

➡ What resources and individuals are there on your college campus that will help you manage your business?

Choosing Your Business Team

An important part of being a successful manager is recognizing what to look for in potential employees as well as being able to delegate tasks and responsibility. You want to hire people who will have the same work ethics and attitude that you have built your business on. A slacker will slow down the growth of your business, degrade the quality of the product or service you are offering, and lower morale. Every person who works for you is a direct reflection on your business. It is extremely important that these people share your values and treat the business with respect.

The business team you build will be the backbone of your business. Selecting the right type of people who will have a positive impact on your business is essential to the success of the venture. Potential investors will be just as interested in the quality of your business team as in your business idea. Look for people who have the right type of personal attributes and qualities that will help create a stimulating and enthusiastic work environment. Each person who is involved with your business will have an impact on the operations of the venture, so be scrupulous when hiring.

Being close friends with someone does not mean that they will make good business partners. Sometimes working with friends can be very difficult. It is more important that a business associate have similar goals, ambitions, and personality traits than that they be your best friend.

Assess the weaknesses of your business and determine which areas you need to enhance. Then look for individuals who have the necessary skills to fill these voids as part of your business team. One of the greatest advantages of college is the diverse student body surrounding you. Take advantage of the skills of these individuals and learn from their experiences.

As the head of a business, it is critical that you supervise the work of others to assure the quality of work being performed. Just because you may think individuals are very smart does not ensure that they will be hard workers. Always inquire about previous working positions and check references on potential employees before you hire them. Even if it means just talking with some of your other friends who know the person, it is of utmost importance to make sure that your business does not have any slackers.

➡ What characteristics and skills are important to you in prospective team members?

➡ What weaknesses are there in your business team and how can you improve them?

After Hiring

Once you do hire individuals with a variety of skills that can help your business in different ways, give them the freedom to test their ideas and make suggestions on different ways of doing things. This will allow your business to operate as if it were twice as large with half the people.

It is imperative to make everyone involved in the business feel that they are important and make a valuable contribution. Give each team member a reason to care about the success of your business. Establish a program in which each employee gets a certain percentage of every sale he or she is responsible for. Encourage new ideas from the people you work with. These new ideas will become instrumental in new initiatives for your business. Employees who feel they are a critical part of the success of your business will work harder for you.

Rather than addressing the people working for you as employees, refer to them as partners, associates, business team members, or some other way to make them feel they are an integral part of your company. Many times you will all be of a similar age, and some people may feel uncomfortable working for another individual their age. To overcome this, create a cohesive team unit that has a good time and enjoys what they are doing. The more fun you have as a group, the more each individual will look forward to working every day.

➡ How will you give your business team members an incentive to work toward the success of the business?

Alternatives to Hiring

Beginning your business will require a wide range of activities. You may be called upon to design a logo, develop a Web site, comprehend highly technical information, understand financial statements, answer phones, manufacture a product, take legal action, and a plethora of other tasks. Not all of these require that you hire someone to fulfill them. Rather, it is often a better idea to outsource some of these tasks.

For example, if you have a friend who is a graphic designer, have them develop the logo for your business. If another one of your friends is an expert at designing Web pages, have him or her help your business establish an online presence. Rather than hire legal help when you are ready to incorporate, use the sites on the Web that will incorporate your business for anywhere from $100 to $300, such as Corporate Agents (www.incorporate.com) or Harvard Business Services (www.delawareinc.com).

Try communicating by e-mail as much as possible to alleviate the need for someone to answer the phones, or get a voice mailbox that you can retrieve messages from. Find different ways of paying your friends. Have a big party for them, or offer them special discounts on the products or service you are offering. Some friends may be willing to help your business for free because they can put the experience on their résumé.

There are many ways to efficiently handle the numerous tasks involved with running a business. The goal is to have your business run as smoothly as possible, allowing you to oversee the operations as a whole.

Utilizing Your Resources

You are surrounded by resources that can help your business run more efficiently, so take advantage of them. You can't be an expert on everything; instead, use the resources that you have in your university and your local community as well as friends and parents.

The University

College universities offer many resources that are helpful when starting a business. One of the greatest assets you have as a collegiate entrepreneur is the university and the individuals and facilities that comprise it. Taking advantage of resources such as campus libraries, faculty, and the diverse student body will give your business an edge in the marketplace.

Campus officials try to create the best possible living environment for their students. Therefore, if your product or service makes their lives better, they may be interested in helping. The university can be a big asset for your business if you take the time to work with them and create a mutually beneficial arrangement. It is important to ensure that you comply with all university rules and regulations if your business involves any sort of campus property, student groups, or any other university sponsored entity.

Remember not to confine yourself to just your school. Use the Internet to branch out to include team members at other universities across the nation. Incorporate them into your business team and have them explore the resources available at their college. Take advantage of all the resources their school offers as well, and use them to build a solid foundation for your business nationwide.

University faculty represent one of the best resources available to you and your business. Almost all professors have office hours to meet to discuss issues students may have, even if they are not specifically related to their class. And even if you are not enrolled in one of their classes, many professors will kindly take the time to meet with you to discuss an idea or question you may have. All professors have achieved the required level of education and experience necessary to hold such a prestigious teaching position. Their experiences and knowledge will prove invaluable to you as you begin to build your business.

Spend time with different professors to learn from them and apply the knowledge to your own business. Whether you confer with an English professor over the grammar in your business plan or get a finance professor to help you prepare the financial statements, professors can help with various aspects of starting your venture.

They may also have valuable connections for you on other campuses or in the corporate world. As long as you are prepared when you meet with them and are appreciative of their help, they will often go out of their way to help you and your business. If certain members are particularly helpful, you may want to offer them more of a role in your business, if they are interested, such as a place on your advisory board. Having experienced people to consult with will help you make intelligent business decisions as you grow.

➡ How does your business make the lives of college students better?

➡ Does it make sense to offer your product or service at other college campuses?

➡ What people do you know at other colleges who would make valuable members of your business team?

➡ What professors specialize in subjects applicable to the business you are starting?

➡ Have any of these professors started a business in the same industry?

➡ Is there an entrepreneurial department at your school?

Friends

Friends can be a big help when starting a business. Whether they lend an extra hand when things are busy or are official members of the business team, you can almost always trust and count on friends. As stated earlier, if you do start a business with your friends, it is essential to make sure you both share the same goals and ambitions for the business. Do not let the business be detrimental to your relationships.

Always put everything in writing. Even if this individual is your closest friend, having a written record will avoid confusion and aggravation in the future. Just look at it as a simple rule of business and a necessary step in laying the proper foundation for your venture.

➡ Which friends of yours, if any, do you plan on incorporating into your business team?

Parents

A lot of your friends at college have parents who have valuable experience in the business world. Investigate whether any of your friends' parents have professions that are complementary to your business venture. Speak with them and learn from their experiences and advice. They may even be able to help you by putting you in touch with other industry contacts.

The more people you talk to about your business, the more you will learn. Running a business is a never-ending learning process. There are always new things to learn and experiences to benefit from. By speaking with the parents of your friends and learning from their experiences and knowledge, you will give yourself an advantage that will benefit you through college into your adult years.

➡ What parents of your friends have experience in an industry complementary to yours?

➡ What advice can they give you on your business idea?

The Community

The local community is often overlooked and overshadowed by the events associated with the university and campus life. Nevertheless, there can be opportunities embedded in the local community for your business to take advantage of. Whether you are in the middle of

Nebraska or in the heart of New York City, there are resources available to your business somewhere nearby. These can include a local Small Business Administration (SBA) office, which can provide loans and counseling, the Chamber of Commerce, and the library.

Introduce yourself to local business owners and explain your business idea. Look for alumni of your school who reside in the area. Learn about the businesses and individuals in your community, and make a point to become familiar with them and to seek their advice.

Resources are all around you, and it is up to you to take advantage of them. You never know what sort of opportunities or joint ventures may be waiting around the corner. Taking advantage of every resource available to you is one of the keys to succeeding in entrepreneurship.

➡ What local businesses and professions in your area could you meet with?

➡ Are there any alumni living in the area who have experience and connections that would help you?

➡ Besides the ones noted here, what other resources can you think of that would help you when starting your business?

Main Points

Managing a business is like caring for a baby; it always needs your attention. However, by using all available resources and getting the most out of your employees, it will free you up to spend more time on other tasks. Consider the following points as you create and learn to manage your organization.

• Take the time to assess the needs of your business and build the proper foundation so that it can handle growth when your business takes off.

• Look for business team members who are hard workers and share your beliefs and values.

• Encourage each business team member to come up with new ideas and give them an incentive to help the company in any way possible.

• Utilize your university, friends, parents, and the local community as valuable resources to help your business.

Use the organizational structure and employee application worksheets at the end of this chapter as a way to brainstorm about your ideal candidates and to screen potential employees. Then use the tasks and resources worksheet to make sure you cover all the sources of help available to your business.

Interview

Professor Tom Byers

Stanford Technology Venture Partners, Stanford University, Stanford, California, interviewed by the author, October 27, 1998

Q: How did you become interested in teaching entrepreneurship?

A: Up until five years ago, I really didn't think about teaching entrepreneurship. I was just an entrepreneurial practitioner: a general manager, corporate officer, executive, and all that stuff. I really was obsessed with the development of our professionals and specifically our young engineers. I often found that they lacked certain skills that they should have, especially the young ones who hadn't had a lot of work experience. They might understand a lot of the technology very well and even the industry very well, but they often lacked leadership qualities, what we now term entrepreneurial leadership qualities.

Q: Once you saw the vision of teaching entrepreneurship, what were your next steps?

A: At this point I was definitely interested, and I knew that you could teach entrepreneurship as a process, as long as you see it as a way of leading and a way of managing. It turns out that this is the way that most people see Silicon Valley, not necessarily as a haven of technology but as a way of doing business. So it's all under this umbrella of entrepreneurial leadership as defined as seizing opportunities. So with that in mind, seeing it as a process, it became clear to me that this was something I'd like to sink my teeth into.

Q: Why did you choose to teach at Stanford?

A: Its location in Silicon Valley, its entrepreneurial legacy, and its technological history made it a perfect prototype, the perfect place to think about these issues. Out of anywhere in the world, this is probably ground zero. It was the ideal location, the ideal petri dish. Stanford and Silicon Valley for the last 50 years have had this really warm relationship. It's been symbiotic; it's been one plus one equals three.

Q: How did Stanford Technology Venture Partners (STVP) become a program and not just a collection of courses?

A: It was very incremental. At first we said, "Look, we think we have something here. We think there's certainly a big need out there to properly introduce and expose engineers to the entrepreneurship process while they're in school." We felt clear about that. So we decided to pilot a couple of ideas.

Q: You have mentioned the incredible student interest in entrepreneurship and STVP. How much of the interest in the student aspect of the program has to do with being located in Silicon Valley?

A: I think it's going on everywhere. As I've gotten to know other campuses in the last two or three years, I've found that there's a healthy dose of religious fervor about entrepreneurship everywhere, at every major school in any region of the country. Also, based on our contacts and interest from our international friends, it's growing worldwide.

Others may see Stanford and Silicon Valley as the center of gravity, which is very flattering, but I tend to believe that the important point here regarding STVP is that you can have a wide range of activities anywhere. You can do it with a lean staff, as far as regular faculty goes, if you can divide it up and get a set of things that faculty can lead, such as leading research and designing courses and so forth. Then they can get help from consulting faculty. But then you also have to make sure to give the students a chance to participate in leading activities, not just participating in activities. They'll come up with some amazing ideas.

Organizational Structure

President _____

Chief Financial Officer _____

Chief Operational Officer _____

Vice President of Sales _____

Sales Force

_____
_____
_____
_____

Administrative Force

_____
_____
_____
_____

Work Force

_____
_____
_____
_____

Advisory Board

_____
_____
_____
_____

Notes _____

_____
_____
_____
_____
_____
_____

Employee Application Form

Name _____   Social Security Number _____

Street address _____   Apt. no. _____

City _____   State _____   Zip _____

Telephone _____   E-mail address _____

Have you served any time in the military? _____

Have you ever been convicted of a crime? _____

Education

Name of school _____   Location _____

Did you graduate? _____   Last grade completed _____

Additional education or classes _____

_____

Work Experience

Company _____   Position _____

Salary _____   Dates employed _____

Job supervisor _____   Reason for leaving _____

Company _____   Position _____

Salary _____   Dates employed _____

Job supervisor _____   Reason for leaving _____

Personal References

Name _____   Phone number _____

Name _____   Phone number _____

What interests you about the job you are applying for?

_____

_____

_____

_____

Notes _____

_____

_____

_____

_____

_____

_____

Tasks and Resources

Tasks owners can do

_____

_____

_____

_____

Tasks needing assistance

_____

_____

_____

_____

Tasks needing hired help

_____

_____

_____

_____

Tasks to outsource

_____

_____

_____

_____

University
Faculty
Friends at your college
Friends at other colleges
Parents
Local community

Notes

_____

_____

_____

_____

_____

_____

_____

_____

Part III

Financial, Legal, and Tax Issues

The Financial Plan

Legal and Tax Issues

Chapter 7

The Financial Plan

Skills such as managing finances and dealing with all types of stake-holders can be developed much earlier when college students start a business.

Robert D. Hisrich, Ph.D.
Case Western Reserve University Entrepreneurial Chair.

Preparing a Successful and Easy-to-use Financial Plan

A financial plan is an outline of the capital it will take to start and run your business. The key to any financial plan is to make realistic assumptions and expectations for your business. It is very easy to underestimate the amount of money and resources involved in starting a business. However, if you take the time to carefully analyze the operations and structure of the business, you will be able to make fairly accurate estimates. According to Jonathan Kleiman, a registered financial advisor with Prudential Securities in New York, budgeting is like dieting; it takes an eternity to get started, and once you do it, it usually doesn't last. But don't give up. Like dieting, planning for the finances of your business is not always fun at first, yet the rewards can be quite gratifying. (Kleiman 1998)

Starting a business often requires making some sacrifices. Whether it is staying in on a Friday night or simply saving all of your change in a jar, if you start to save now, it is much more likely you will have the capital you need when you need it. Just $25 a week, growing at 10 percent annualized interest, will equal close to $3,000 by the end of your second year. (Kleiman 1998)

According to annual statistics from the Small Business Administration, one of the major causes of small business failure is lack of financial understanding and undercapitalization. No matter how big or small your business is, it is essential to properly establish a projected balance sheet, income statement, and statement of cash flows. It is also a good idea to create a worksheet that details your start-up costs and break-even analysis.

Preparing the financial statements is a somewhat tedious, yet necessary, step in the financial plan. Do not be intimidated if you have not had any experience in this area. It is an excellent learning exercise and is not as difficult as you may think. The worksheets at the end of this chapter will help you establish the financial statements for your business. If you are still having trouble understanding the concepts of the financial statements, speak with a finance or accounting professor. It is also a good idea to take a general accounting or finance class.

Learning to do financial statements is an invaluable skill that you will use over and over in the business world. Realize that it is just as important to understand the logic behind the financial statements as it is to fill in the numbers in the blanks. These documents will help you understand the amount of money your business will require to start up, operate, and grow. By properly preparing the financial statements, you will be able to comprehend the logic and meaning behind the numbers.

➡ Have you had experience with preparing balance sheets, income statements, or cash flow projections?

➡ Who can you speak with for advice regarding a financial plan for your business?

Start-up Costs

Establishing a financial plan is a necessary step in beginning any business. No matter how large or small your business is, it is extremely important to analyze the different expenses you will incur and the anticipated revenue you will earn. The goal is to keep your expenses low and generate a high profit margin on products or services rendered.

There are inevitable costs associated with starting any type of business. The key to keeping expenses low is to take advantage of all the resources available to you. For example, some legal, financial, tax, and marketing professionals may be willing to advise your company for free now in exchange for a piece of the glory to come or an agreement to act as consultants once you have the money to pay them. (Pierce 1998) At college you have an incredible pool of resources that are not available to most entrepreneurs. These can include free Web pages, financial and legal advice from professors, and low-cost advertising in your school newspaper and bulletins. Using these resources will help keep your expenses low and increase your bottom line.

The worksheet at the end of this chapter will list some of the potential costs you will have when starting your business. Of course, there may be other expenses that you incur, depending on the type of business you are in.

With the advent of e-mail and the World Wide Web, there are new ways to carry on business that were not available only a few years ago. By putting your company online via a Web site, you can have a virtual storefront for a fraction of the cost associated with a brick and mortar establishment. In addition, e-mail allows you to converse with customers without the need for a dedicated phone line and a person to answer the phone. Creating an online store also allows you to be open 24 hours a day to potential customers all over the world.

If you want to have a phone number, you can set up a voice mailbox with a local telecommunications company. For between $5 and $15 a month, you can get a voice mailbox with a direct phone number. Then, for slightly more, you can be paged whenever you receive a new message.

These are just a few examples of the ways technological advances have created new opportunities for entrepreneurs. (See the entrepreneurial resources guide in Chapter 11 for others.) These resources in addition to the ones available on campus create a dynamic opportunity for your entrepreneurial ambitions.

➡ What start-up expenses do you anticipate?

➡ How much will these cost?

➡ What resources can you take advantage of to alleviate some start-up costs?

Break-even Analysis

The break-even point is when a business's income is equal to its expenses. It is an exciting day for every business when it goes into the black, otherwise known as becoming profitable. It is common to expect that it may take many months or even longer before your business becomes profitable. It is important to calculate this break-even point so that you have enough start-up funds to continue operating for the first couple of slow months.

Some companies operate in the red for many years before they become profitable. This does not mean that they are not worth anything in the marketplace but rather that their expenses are more than their sales. Until recently, it was rumored that Amazon.com, the large online bookseller, was not making any money; however, they are worth billions of dollars and are using a lot of their cash to fuel growth, create a brand image, and employ extensive advertising.

Depending on the goals and ambitions for your business, you should forecast projected earnings for the first couple of months. It is always a good idea to retain some of the earnings your business accumulates to help expand your business and to use when business is slow, such as during holidays and term breaks. Proper planning and cash flow projections will help push your company into the black and foster timely growth and profitability.

- ➡ At what point do you expect your business to reach the break-even point and begin making money?
- ➡ How do you plan to use the proceeds from your business?

Income Statement

The income statement reports the profit or loss for your business for a given period of time. It is also called the profit and loss statement, or P&L. Basically, it compares the revenues and expenses of your business. Revenues are the monies received for goods and services rendered. Expenses are the costs associated with generating the revenue. Net income is the difference between the two. The income statement reports the activities of your business over a period of time, such as a year, and is often used to represent changes from year to year in retained earnings, which is money that is reinvested in the business. The income statement shows investors the changes in the amount of retained earnings being held onto by the business.

Sample Income Statement and Retained Earnings

Jake's Fruit Smoothies, Inc.
Income Statement and Retained Earnings
For the Year Ending December 31, 1998

Revenues	$12,000
Less expenses	7,000
Net income	5,000
Retained earnings, January 1, 1997	1,500
Total	6,500
Less dividends declared	3,000
Retained earnings, December 31, 1998	$ 3,500

➡ What are the expected revenues of your business?

➡ What are your expected expenses?

➡ Do you expect to have any retained earnings?

Balance Sheet

The balance sheet is the statement of financial position for your business at a specific moment in time. The balance sheet is composed of assets, liabilities, and stockholders' equity. The rule of thumb for the balance sheet is that assets equal liabilities plus stockholders' equity. These two sides of the balance sheet must always be equal. Both the assets and liabilities are broken down into current and long-term time frames.

Current assets generally are cash or will become cash within one year. Current liabilities are bills that must be paid within the year. Current assets and liabilities are usually located at the top of the balance sheet to grab the reader's attention. Long-term assets can involve the company's property, plant, and equipment (PPE). These assets are usually held onto for the longer term of greater than one year. Long-term liabilities are usually expenses that are due in the long term, or beyond one year.

Stockholders' equity represents the contributed capital and retained earnings of the company. Contributed capital is the amount of money people have invested in the company for shares of ownership, such as stock. Retained earnings is the portion of income that has not been paid out to the shareholders through dividends. Retained earnings are not actually assets but are a claim on the portion of the assets, like all equity-side entries on the balance sheet.

The specific time when the balance sheet is created is at the end of the company's fiscal year. For the first year of your business, use the calendar year end, December 31. After that, you can establish when you want your year end to be. It is usually a good idea to have it at a slow point in the year so that you can spend some extra time preparing your financial statements.

Sample Balance Sheet

Jake's Fruit Smoothies, Inc.
Balance Sheet
December 31, 1998

Assets

Current assets	$ 8,000
Fixed assets	3,000
Investments	2,000
Other	500
Total assets	$13,500

Liabilities and Shareholders' Equity

Liabilities	$ 2,000
Current liabilities	5,000
Long-term liabilities	7,000
Stockholders' equity Investments	3,000
Retained earnings	3,500
Total stockholders' equity	6,500
Total liabilities and stockholders' equity	$13,500

➥ What current and long-term assets will your business have?
➥ What current and long-term liabilities will your business have?
➥ Will you have any retained earnings?

Statement of Cash Flows

The statement of cash flows depicts where cash resources came from and how they are used. It explains changes in the working capital of your business. Working capital refers to items such as cash, inventory, and other current assets. Net working capital is derived by subtracting current liabilities from current assets.

The statement of cash flows has come to be required only in the last 15 years or so. It provides more substantial information about the cash inflow and outflow of a business. Specifically, the statement of cash flows provides better information than the income statement and balance sheet do about the liquidity of your business, meaning the amount of cash your business can produce at any given moment. The statement of cash flows will also show you how much money is needed to start your venture and keep it running. A good rule of thumb is to have at least enough capital to run for the first two or three months with very few sales.

Sample Statement of Cash Flows

Jake's Fruit Smoothies, Inc.
Statement of Cash Flows
For the Year Ending December 31, 1998

Cash Generated from Operating Activities	
Customers	$11,000
Payments	(4,000)
Net cash from operating activities	$ 7,000
Cash Generated from Investing Activities	
Property, plant, and equipment	$ 3,000
Net cash from investing activities	($ 3,000)
Cash Generated from Financing Activities	
Borrowing from creditors	$ 1,000
Stock	1,500
Net cash from financing activities	$ 2,500
Cash Net Increase or Decrease	$ 6,500
Cash at beginning of year	2,500
Cash at end of year	$ 9,000

➡ What will be your cash intake and output from operating activities, investing activities, and financing activities for the year?

➡ What will be your cash balance at the beginning of the year?

Record Keeping

Record keeping is an extremely important part of starting a business. Keeping thorough notes of all transactions and conversations and doing the financial statements on a monthly basis will give you much better control in managing your business. In addition, this will be extremely helpful in identifying problem areas and strengths in your business. For example, if you see that customers are paying mostly by credit card, you may want to offer a discount to those who pay cash because you pay a percentage to the credit card companies of each sale charged.

As you begin your business, you will become inundated with papers, e-mail, and random notes that will be important to your business. If you fail to keep it all organized, critical information such as loan payments could become neglected and you run the risk of ruining your business. It is also a good idea to begin keeping track of the individuals you speak with about your business. These people may prove to be valuable contacts, and it is important to keep up with them. Computer programs such as ACT, a client management software, will organize your lists of customers, potential customers, advisors, and other contacts and help you keep track of your conversations with them.

Take the time now before you get too busy to establish a filing system and other organizational methods that will enable you to be much more prepared when you become busier as your business grows. Organized people are able to operate at a much higher level of efficiency and undertake a considerably greater amount of work than unorganized and unprepared individuals. Take advantage of this opportunity now to enhance your operational output.

➡ What files, notes, e-mail, and other papers will you need to organize on a regular basis?

➡ How do you plan to file these pieces of information?

➡ How will you record your contacts and make sure you keep in touch with them?

Potential Investors

Both lenders and investors are concerned with whether or not you have what it takes to be successful. In your financial plan, highlight information that demonstrates you have the ability to make this business a success. Detail your education and past successes or failures that made you stronger. Indicate how you started the business and what makes you believe it will be a success.

To be a successful entrepreneur, you must not only be able to start well but also to finish strong. Good management is essential. Funding sources desire to see that you understand your market and have the skills to succeed. Give detailed résumés of all those involved, along with a description of the vital roles they will play in the business's success. If your management skills or your business team is weak, take on the task of building it up in order to support your own success, as well as the success of your funding request.

Listen to good advice and forget bad counsel. Carefully seek out and select professionals to advise you. Do your homework well in advance of your need for funding so as to avoid delays. (Pierce 1998)

The increasing number of financing choices available to entrepreneurs can seem very confusing. It is important to determine your financial objectives and to understand your current financial position, risk tolerance, and financing alternatives. It is always good to keep in mind the long-term objectives of your business, even though you may just be starting out. (Kleiman 1998)

There are many different groups of people who invest in companies. Whether you tap into your own personal savings, credit cards, friends, parents, venture capitalists, loan officers, or angel investors, there are a plethora of people who finance start-up and small businesses. Depending on the amount of money you need to raise, certain groups will be more likely to consider providing you with capital. Each group has different requirements and regulations for use of their money. The goal is to fit your company's needs with the right type of financing.

The ideal way to finance your business is to use your own money. If you are starting a business on a small scale, it is best to finance it on your own, using the resources around you, a limited amount of money, and a lot of creativity. It is also important to note that investors like to see that you have invested your own money in your business. This proves you believe in your concept enough to back it with your own money. If you do not want to tap in to your personal savings or do not have the extra cash, there are certainly other options. However, if you are starting a small business and can keep your expenses low enough to afford financing it on your own, it is definitely your best bet.

If you are personally financing the venture, you do not want to have to continue putting in so much money that it affects your own personal finances. If you decide to get outside financing, you will need to determine whether you seek debt or equity financing. Debt financing is when you take out a loan, whether from a bank or even your parents. You pay back parts of the loan, the principal plus interest over a predetermined time period. Equity financing is when investors put money into your business in return for an ownership position in the company. The right combination of debt and equity financing will depend on the size and scale of the business you are starting.

Financing your business via your friends or parents or other family members can get complicated. Parents are often a great source of financing because you can borrow money from them with little or no interest. They may even give you part of the money because they are glad you are taking the initiative to start an entrepreneurial venture. Although this option may seem very attractive, if not established on the right terms, it can create friction in the future. Always be upfront with your friends or family members, and always put everything in writing. The more official you keep your documents, the easier all your dealings with your funders will be later.

If you have a limited credit history, it can be difficult to obtain a bank loan. Loans for starting a business are different from any student loans for tuition that you may already have. Loan officers usually require a minimum of a few years of credit history or some form of collateral in order to obtain a loan. Although this may be difficult, if you are able to obtain a loan, it will help establish your credit history and make it easier to obtain additional financing in the future.

Another possible source of loans is the Small Business Administration (SBA). The SBA is a government-sponsored program that offers financing assistance, in addition to many other services, to small business owners and entrepreneurs. Each year they make investments in start-up businesses and in small businesses that need additional capital. The guidelines for funding differ for each type of loan, so visit an SBA office or their Web site (www.sba.gov) to look into the available options.

Credit cards represent another source of financing for your business. This should not be the first choice to finance your venture, however, because most college students are inexperienced in dealing with easy debt and compounding high interest rates. While there have been success stories of businesses started on credit cards, the failures have not been as well publicized. Most college students receive offers for credit cards without even applying for them. If you do use credit cards, be very careful to manage the debt wisely and pay it off as soon as possible.

Angel investors are wealthy individuals who invest in different business opportunities. They are dubbed angels because they often invest money with reasonable terms and understand the ups and downs of starting a business. Angel investors are also attractive because they often have had previous experience with starting businesses and can sometimes provide you with guidance and industry contacts to help open doors for your company. Yet not every angel investor provides the most simple terms when investing their money. Each situation and individual you deal with is unique.

It should be your goal to find the best combination of investor capital, terms, and willingness to help. One place to look is ACE-NET, another service offered by the SBA, which matches entrepreneurs with accredited investors having a net worth of greater than $500,000.

- ➡ Will you be able to personally finance your business?
- ➡ If not, how do you plan to finance your business?
- ➡ What type of funders are you the most comfortable with?
- ➡ What do you see as the strengths and weaknesses associated with each?
- ➡ What combination of debt and equity do you want for your business?

Venture Capital

According to Josh Rappoport, a venture capitalist for Summit Partners in Boston, venture capital (VC) is an excellent source of financing, if you can get it. Venture capitalists are professional investors who give money to entrepreneurs in order to help start or expand a business. In return, venture capitalists usually receive an equity stake, or percentage ownership, in the company. Typically, VC firms invest in high-growth industries and in companies that have particular competitive advantages within those industries. Those companies that receive venture capital, also called venture-backed companies, must show the potential to generate tens if not hundreds of millions of dollars. Do not, however, let this intimidate you. You need look only as far as Internet companies Yahoo! and Excite to find other collegiate entrepreneurs who were able to attract venture capitalists to fund a company with extraordinary worth.

Venture capital is more than just money. As partial owners, or shareholders, of the business, venture capitalists are motivated to help their companies succeed. VC firms will use their experience with other companies in a similar stage of development or in similar industries to help guide your company strategically. They may be able to provide invaluable contacts with other companies that will act as suppliers, customers, or partners. They may even provide personnel to help aid management in key business areas such as marketing, sales, or product development.

Aside from having a claim to the financial worth of the company, VCs demand that they have certain controls and that the management team of the company be accountable to them. As an entrepreneur, you may find that the controls inhibit your creativity and style or you may welcome the more structured and controlled business environment.

Lastly, venture capitalists will also act as cheerleaders trying to help you position your company for success. These are generalizations, however, and VC firms each approach their role in a slightly different way. Be sure to understand what you want and what you will get from your particular investors and partners before you enter an agreement with them. (Rappoport 1998)

There are many venture capital companies all over the world. To contact them, try some of the Web sites now devoted to venture capital, such as Vfinance.com (www.vfinance.com) or FinanceHub (www.financehub.com).

Should you decide to seek venture capital, be prepared for rejection and lots of it. Gaining an audience is not an easy matter, and you may have to try contacting 10 or more venture capital firms before one will be willing to speak with you. You may have to revise your business plan several times before you have it just right. Do not give up, and do not get discouraged. Just as in life, you must use every setback as a learning experience that will propel you and your business forward. It only takes one investor to help launch your company on the path to stardom; if you steadfastly believe in yourself and your business, you are sure to find a way to accomplish your goals. (Rappoport 1998)

Venture capital is not for all entrepreneurs or all businesses. It is a difficult process and one that is not appropriate for everyone. Growing a business through your own hard work and sweat equity, maintaining 100 percent ownership and control, and becoming a great success is perhaps the ideal outcome of an entrepreneurial endeavor. However, this is not always possible or appropriate. If, through your research, you find that your company is well positioned to receive venture backing and that your business can significantly benefit from this type of investment, do not hesitate to explore these opportunities. (Rappoport 1998)

➡ Do you have a business idea that could yield substantial enough rewards to be interesting to venture capitalists?

➡ Are you comfortable giving up partial ownership of your business in return for equity?

Main Points

Creating a financial plan is a necessary step that forces you to understand what it takes to start, operate, and expand your business. Consider these points when creating the financial plan for your venture.

- Take the time to learn how to prepare a balance sheet, income statement, and statement of cash flows.
- Use realistic assumptions and expectations when preparing your financial statements.
- Make sure you have enough capital to operate for the first two to three months when business is slow.
- At college you are surrounded with resources that you can leverage to keep your expenses low and your profits high.
- Maintain good credit and establish relations with the bank and other possible funding sources.
- Always have an idea of where you can get more capital if your business needs it.

Use the projected start-up costs and financing sources worksheets at the end of this chapter to begin getting a grip on the finances of your venture. Then use the balance sheet, income statement, and cash flow worksheets to create financial projections for your business.

Interview

Professor Robert D. Hisrich, Ph.D.

Chair in Entrepreneurial Studies, Case Western Reserve University, Cleveland, Ohio, interviewed by the author, October 10, 1998

Q: Tell me about your background.

A: I have had industry experience with three major Fortune 500 companies, Ford Motor Company, Proctor & Gamble, and Hillenbrand Industries, and have been involved in the start-up of numerous business ventures. I have academic degrees and taught entrepreneurship at Massachusetts Institute of Technology, the University of Tulsa, and Case Western Reserve University. I currently hold the Mixon Chair of Entrepreneurial Studies at the Weatherhead School of Management at Case Western Reserve University.

Q: How did you get interested in entrepreneurship?

A: I have always loved to create and to observe entrepreneurs having fun creating and developing their ideas. The area followed nicely on my research and work in the area of marketing and product planning and development.

Q: What do you feel is the most challenging aspect of starting and owning your own business?

A: The most challenging aspect is to come up with a unique product or service that has appeal to a large enough market niche and then to put together a plan to successfully access that market cost effectively.

Q: What do you find is the most rewarding aspect?

A: Having the freedom and independence to do what you like to do and being able to create and grow something new that you believe in.

Q: What resources do you find are helpful when starting a business?

A: The most helpful resources are advice concerning the market niche, the capital structure of the new venture, and other legal and organizational issues.

Q: What advice would you give college students on starting their own business?

A: Be sure you have a product or service that is unique and that you define its unique differential advantages and its market niche. Do not think you can be all things to all people.

Q: What do you feel entrepreneurs can learn from starting a business in college?

A: A critical understanding of the creating process and what it takes to start, develop, and manage in a business environment. Skills such as managing finances and dealing with all types of stakeholders can be developed much earlier when college students start a business.

Q: What have been some of the most interesting student ideas and projects that you have witnessed?

A: A few of the most unusual ones include a bed and breakfast inn in Croatia, a dinner and dancing entertainment boat, a children's wheelchair that looked like a small car, a delivery service for gourmet food, a new medical monitoring device, and a method for delivering high quality multimedia content over the Internet.

Q: What are your general thoughts on entrepreneurship?

A: Entrepreneurship provides the opportunity to learn all about managing in today's hypercompetitive world and to have a real feeling of accomplishment.

Projected Start-up Costs

Company _____

Owner _____

Graphic design	$_____
Legal assistance	$_____
Inventory	$_____
Bank account	$_____
Hiring advertisements	$_____
Communication devices	$_____
Marketing	$_____
Letterhead	$_____
Salary	$_____
Supplies	$_____
Equipment	$_____
Insurance	$_____
Office space	$_____
Storage space	$_____
License fees	$_____
Other	$_____
Total	$_____

Financing Sources

Capital needed to start business $_____

Capital needed for first three months of business $_____

Total capital needed $_____

Preferred type of debt or equity financing   ___% debt   ___% equity

Potential Sources	Estimated Amount	Type of Financing
Personal funds	$_____	_____
Parents	$_____	_____
Family members	$_____	_____
Friends	$_____	_____
Bank	$_____	_____
SBA	$_____	_____
Angel investors	$_____	_____
Venture capital	$_____	_____
Other	$_____	_____

Contacts

_____

_____

_____

_____

_____

_____

Notes

_____

_____

_____

_____

_____

_____

_____

_____

Projected Balance Sheet
End of First Year

Assets

Current assets

Cash	$_____
Accounts receivable	$_____
Merchandise inventory	$_____
Supplies	$_____
Total current assets	$

Fixed assets

Property, plant, and equipment	$_____
Less depreciation	$_____
Total fixed assets	$
Total assets	$_____

Liabilities and Owner's equity

Current liabilities

Accounts payable	$_____
Current portion of long-term debt	$_____
Total current liabilities	$

Long-term liabilities

Notes payable	$_____
Other long-term liabilities	$_____
Total long-term liabilities	$

Owner's equity

Personal	$_____
First investor	$_____
Second investor	$_____
Retained earnings	$_____
Total owner's equity	$
Total liabilities and owner's equity	$_____

Projected Income Statement

	Month											
	1	2	3	4	5	6	7	8	9	10	11	12
33% of estimated revenues	—	—	—	—	—	—	—	—	—	—	—	—
50% of estimated revenues	—	—	—	—	—	—	—	—	—	—	—	—
100% of estimated revenues	—	—	—	—	—	—	—	—	—	—	—	—
Start-up costs	—	—	—	—	—	—	—	—	—	—	—	—
Advertising	—	—	—	—	—	—	—	—	—	—	—	—
Salaries	—	—	—	—	—	—	—	—	—	—	—	—
Benefits	—	—	—	—	—	—	—	—	—	—	—	—
Telephone	—	—	—	—	—	—	—	—	—	—	—	—
Web site	—	—	—	—	—	—	—	—	—	—	—	—
Rent	—	—	—	—	—	—	—	—	—	—	—	—
Credit card processing	—	—	—	—	—	—	—	—	—	—	—	—
Other	—	—	—	—	—	—	—	—	—	—	—	—
33% revenue operating income	—	—	—	—	—	—	—	—	—	—	—	—
Year-to-date revenue	—	—	—	—	—	—	—	—	—	—	—	—
50% revenue operating income	—	—	—	—	—	—	—	—	—	—	—	—
Year-to-date revenue	—	—	—	—	—	—	—	—	—	—	—	—
100% revenue operating income	—	—	—	—	—	—	—	—	—	—	—	—
Year-to-date revenue	—	—	—	—	—	—	—	—	—	—	—	—

Assumptions

Projected Statement of Cash Flows

Month

	1	2	3	4	5	6	7	8	9	10	11	12
33% of estimated revenue												
50% of estimated revenue												
100% of estimated revenue												
Monthly expenses												
33% revenue cash flow												
33% revenue cumulative cash flow												
50% revenue cash flow												
50% revenue cumulative cash flow												
100% revenue cash flow												
100% revenue cumulative cash flow												

Assumptions

_____

_____

_____

Chapter 8

Legal and Tax Issues

Accept the fact that you have no experience running a business, which does take skill and practice, and start small, work carefully, and watch for signs of trouble.

Larry Downs and Chunka Mui
Authors of *Unleashing the Killer App*

Legal and Tax Concerns

Legal and tax issues can have a huge impact on the future of your business. Doing your homework now to understand their effects on your business will help alleviate increased work, exposure to liability, and other headaches later on.

The legal and tax issues associated with your business will vary, depending upon the size and type of business you are starting. Regardless, it is a good idea to have an understanding of the general tax and legal implications for your business from the start. Preparing the proper documents will help in building a solid foundation for your business.

Whether to Hire a Lawyer or Accountant

It is not always necessary to hire a professional lawyer or accountant in the beginning stages of your business. It is always recommended that you have professional advice; however, if you are starting a small-scale business that you are operating by yourself, you may be able to postpone these expenses, if you can handle them effectively yourself. Services such as incorporation, for example, can be handled through by online sites like The Company Corporation (www.incorporate.com) or Harvard Business Services (www.delawareinc.com). Another way to avoid extensive legal and accounting fees is to speak with the accounting and law professors at your school. As your business grows, you may need to get professional help to keep things orderly.

Be aware that your business will be exposed to certain risks and liabilities. These may include actions of your employees, premises liability, and client dissatisfaction. There are liabilities that you may never even have thought of. For example, an employer is responsible for an employee's actions when they are within the scope of your employment, such as an auto accident on the way to a cleaning job for your cleaning service. And if you are in a partnership, you are responsible for the actions of your business partners, whether or not you knew about or approved of those actions. Thus it pays to inform yourself about liability issues; taking the proper legal steps now can greatly mitigate your risks later on.

➡ Who can you speak with for legal advice?

➡ Is the type of business you are starting exposed to certain risks and liabilities?

Business Licenses and Fees

When starting a business, there are certain business licenses you must obtain. First you will be required to apply for a federal tax identification number, also called an employee identification number, which the government uses to make sure you are paying your taxes on income and on wages paid to your employees. To obtain a federal tax identification number, go to the Internal Revenue Service Web site, www.irs.gov, and follow the links to federal tax identification number information. This is a very important step and will be a piece of information you need to open a bank account as well.

Some types of businesses are required to obtain licenses for selling food, real estate, and financial advice, just to name a few. Depending on where you are operating your business, you may also be required to pay city, county, or state fees in addition to specific fees based on the type of business you are running. For example, if you are providing real estate advice, depending on where you live, you may have to pay an annual fee in addition to taking a test to obtain a broker's license.

One way to make sure you have all of the licenses is to talk to other individuals with similar businesses in your local area. Ask them what sort of licenses they have, how much they cost, and how frequently they must be renewed. You will find Small Business Development Centers to be helpful, and you can always ask a local small business lawyer. A handy resource for beginning entrepreneurs is the series of books published by Oasis Press called *Smart Start, Your (State) Business* that provides detailed information on each state's licensing requirements as well as taxes, marketing, and other topics.

➡ Have you obtained a federal tax identification number?

➡ What sort of licenses do other similar businesses in your area have?

➡ What are the fees for these licenses?

Copyrights, Patents, and Trademarks

Copyrights protect original works of authorship including art, music, books, photographs, graphic designs, manuals, reports, and computer programs. It is not generally known that you can copyright your work simply by putting the copyright symbol © and your name and the year of creation next to the title of the work. This will save you money and paperwork and is a very easy way to gain immediate protection for your work. However, registering your work with the federal government does provide you with an added layer of protection. This process involves filling out a *Form TX* and paying a fee for processing by the Library of Congress.

Patents are a contract between the United States government and the inventor. The inventor must supply the government with detailed analysis of the invention in addition to other pertinent information. It is important to research your invention against already existing models to ensure you are not infringing on anyone else's previous work. If you are awarded the patent, it protects you from other people using the invention for a specific period of time. The inventor can decide to license the invention to individuals or corporations for a fee and still retain ownership of the patent. After a specified amount of time, the records for the invention become public and anyone can access them. Registering for a patent involves extensive paperwork and a hefty fee of around $1,000 to $1,500, so make sure to do your research and consult with a patent lawyer before you take on this expense.

A trademark is a symbol, saying, design, word, or combination of these that is identified with a certain product or service. Trademarks are filed with the Patent and Trademark Office. Trademarks establish the rights to the material and allow you to put the symbol ® next to the trademarked material. As with copyrights, you are not officially required to register a trademark with the government. Previous use of the trademark gives you legal ownership. Nevertheless, it provides more protection to register the material on a state and national level. Trademarks can cost anywhere from $500 to $1,000, or even more with legal fees, depending on how many states you register in. A trademark is generally used for companies conducting business in several states at once and wanting to ensure protection on a national basis. Consult with a lawyer to help you understand the intricacies of registering for a trademark if you feel the need to gain extra protection for your material.

Legal Structures

The legal form of your business affects your personal tax situation, the company's tax situation, and the liability exposure of you and your business. Selecting the most appropriate legal structure for your business will help to ensure the best possible foundation for your business.

The following descriptions of legal structures are summaries only, meant to give you a basic idea of the positives and negatives of the various types. Speak with a lawyer or a law professor or do some research at the library or online to get more in-depth explanations of the different structures before you decide which one will provide the most benefits for your business.

The basic types of legal structures for your business are:

- Sole proprietorship,
- Partnership,
- Corporation,
- S corporation,
- Limited liability company,
- Limited partnership, and
- Other special cases.

Sole Proprietorship

Your business is automatically a sole proprietorship if you do not have a partner and do not incorporate. This means that you are personally liable for the actions of your business, and the income or loss your business generates is taxed as personal income.

Partnership

The main benefit of forming a partnership is the ability to share the financial burden with your partner or partners. The main risk to forming a partnership is that you are liable for all of your partners' actions, regardless of whether or not you knew about or agreed to their actions. Make sure to get everything in writing when you are dealing with partners.

Corporation

Incorporating your business is a recommended step that provides you and your business with additional legal protection. The main advantage of incorporating is to protect you from liability. Incorporating your business establishes it as an entity by itself and separates the business assets from your own personal assets. This protects your personal assets if there is legal action taken against your business.

The legal steps to form a corporation are not as difficult as you may think. Although laws differ from state to state, there are certain requirements for maintaining corporate status. These include issuing shares of stock in the company, holding shareholders' and directors' meetings at least once a year at which minutes must be taken, paying annual fees to the state, and paying fees to the agent acting as your legal representative. If you transact business in other states, you must qualify to do business in those other states, file the necessary paper-work, and pay the corresponding fees as well.

The disadvantage of corporations is that they are subject to possible double taxation, the first time as corporation taxes and then as personal income taxes if you cash in on profits or sell the business. The worksheet at the end of this chapter will give you an idea of the questions that need to be answered if you decide to incorporate.

S Corporation

An S corporation gives your business liability protection and also allows you to pay taxes as if you were a sole proprietor or in a partnership. S corporations generally do not pay federal income tax but pass through the tax liabilities on profits to the shareholders. An S corporation is generally formed when the corporation distributes almost all of its profits to shareholders or when the shareholders want to take advantage of losses on their personal income tax returns. To qualify, a corporation must have no more than 75 shareholders, have only one class of stock, and may not own 80 percent or more of any other corporation. In many cases, an S corporation is taxed like a partnership, although it may be subject to corporate income tax on a state-by-state basis. Many lawyers recommend this structure for start-up businesses because it reduces your taxes while also providing protection for your business.

Limited Liability Company

A limited liability company (LLC) combines the protection of a corporation and the tax benefits of a partnership. The owners of an LLC have no personal liability for the actions of the LLC but still have personal liability for individual acts in connection with the LLC. An LLC is usually unsuitable for businesses financed by venture capital because of tax restrictions on the fund's tax-exempt partners. The LLC tends to be the choice for startups because losses can be passed through to investors. The LLC is recognized in all 50 states; however, some states require that there be at least two members in the business.

Limited Partnerships

Limited partnerships are generally used for real estate investments or companies envisioning expansion plans. Limited partners are not personally liable for the debts of the business and have identical rights as the general partners; however, they usually cannot hold management positions. Limited partnerships allow small businesses to raise capital without adding new members, issuing stock, or forming a corporate entity.

Other Special Cases

There are also special cases in which other types of legal entities are established. One example is non-profit organizations that are exempt from paying income taxes if they qualify under IRS Section 501 (C)(3). Another example is a professional corporation formed for the sole purpose of offering a professional service, which is shielded from certain liabilities.

No legal entity or insurance program can protect you and your business from all liability. During the normal course of business, there can always be extenuating circumstances beyond your control. The best thing to do is to take all of the steps you can, within reason, to properly shield you and your business before you commence operations. Forming the proper corporate entity for your business and subscribing to some level of insurance, depending on your type of business, will greatly reduce the risk to you personally and to your business.

➡ Which legal structure appears to be the best fit for your business?

➡ What are the benefits of choosing this type of structure?

Tax Issues

There are many tax issues associated with starting a small business. Depending on the legal structure of your business, you will be taxed either personally or as a corporate entity. If you do not form a partnership or you choose not to incorporate, you are automatically considered a sole proprietor, and any earnings you make will be taxed as personal income. If your company is not successful and you lose money, you may be entitled to write off some of the expenses, if you itemize your taxes. It is important to consult with your parents about this if they are still taking care of your taxes for you.

Plan to spend some time and money for the services of a professional accountant to discuss tax issues that will affect your business. The tax laws in existence are numerous, complex, and always changing.

You may be exempt from some and have to pay others. For example, even if your business does not have to pay business property tax, you still have to file annually. Also, do not forget that you must collect sales tax on all products and services that you sell, unless you live in a state with no sales tax.

There are also taxes to be paid if you hire an employee. A business with employees must withhold FICA taxes from employees' wages and forward them to the IRS and the state tax agency. In addition, a business with employees must pay federal and state payroll taxes, the employers' share of FICA, and federal and state unemployment taxes, out of its own pocket. Businesses are also required to obtain workers' compensation insurance for its employees. There are also disabilities programs that have tax implications.

As you can see, there are a multitude of tax issues that affect every business. Do not be intimidated by the vast number of tax issues; just take the time to properly explore those that will affect your business. There are various books that can help you, such as the series called *Smart Start, Your (State) Business* published by Oasis Press, with detailed information by state about taxes and other topics. Other sources of current tax information include the Financial Accounting Standards Board (FASB) at www.fasb.org and the Securities and Exchange Commission (SEC) at www.sec.gov. Take advantage of the resources around you, such as your parents and accounting professors.

In the long run, the best way to deal with taxes is to spend some time with a professional and map out a strategy for your business. Taxes can get extremely complicated, so make sure you consult with someone who has knowledge and experience in preparing taxes for businesses.

➥ What experience do you have with filing taxes?
➥ What tax issues will affect your company?
➥ What are the advantages of the different corporate structures on your tax situation?

Main Points

Legal and tax issues are complex and seem to be in a constant state of change. Therefore, it is extremely important to consult professionals and do thorough research to make sure that you are not overlooking any requirements. Consider the following points when starting your business.

- Decide which legal structure is most appropriate for your business.
- Assess all possible liability and risks that your business may be exposed to.
- Get everything in writing, no matter how trivial it may seem.
- Estimate your taxes on a quarterly basis so you are not surprised with a big tax bill at year end.
- Get the advice of professionals.

Use the legal and tax worksheets at the end of this chapter to prepare yourself for what issues may affect your business.

Interview

Authors Larry Downes and Chunka Mui

Unleashing the Killer App, Harvard Business School Press, 1998. Interview as provided by publisher's press kit materials and as interviewed by the author, July 8, 1998

Larry Downes is a consultant and speaker on the impact of digital technologies on business strategy at Northwestern University, Evanston, Illinois, and with Diamond Technology Partners. Chunka Mui is a partner with Diamond Technology Partners and is the executive editor of the business magazine *Context*.

Digital technology has enabled the Davids of the business world, small companies and entrepreneurs, to directly challenge the large industry leaders: Amazon.com versus the chain bookstore model, Peapod home grocery deliverer versus the traditional grocery store chain, and E*Trade versus the security brokerage powerhouses. The list goes on. The challengers are in many ways better positioned and prepared to take advantage of digital strategy and the unleashing of killer apps. But even the most lumbering Goliath eventually swings its sword. (Downes and Mui 1998)

Q: What is a killer app? What are some recognizable examples?

A: We borrowed the term killer app from the venture capital world in which killer applications, or apps, have long been able to transform industries, unseat market leaders, and provide a thousand-fold return on an initial investment. The spreadsheet was a killer app. It not only quickly transformed the computer industry by making the personal computer popular but also, according to many people, redefined business finance. The 800 number was another killer app. It was created to let citizens suggest inflation-fighting programs as part of President Gerald Ford's Whip Inflation Now (WIN) program. The reversed billing idea caught on so rapidly that over a few years it redefined how people shop and how companies provide customer service. Federal Express, e-mail, the Internet, the World Wide Web, and electronic commerce are examples of other killer apps that are transforming business.

Q: What is fueling the creation of these killer apps?

A: For the most part, the fuel is being supplied by technology advances. In short, the incredible growth of computer processing power and the astonishing expansion of networks, especially the Internet, has set technological change on an exponential pace. But political, social, and economic systems can only change incrementally. The resulting gaps, often filled by entrepreneurs, are the openings for killer apps.

Q: You have said that killer apps are made less often than they are discovered. What do you mean by that?

A: Killer apps are often gold on the floor, ignored because existing players can't recognize their value. Even their inventors rarely understand the full significance of a killer app. The best example of this is probably the Internet itself, a Defense Department construct designed to create a decentralized communications network that could continue to function in the event of some military catastrophe. It wasn't until the Internet got into the hands of entrepreneurs and consumers that its potential began to be realized. Often it takes someone free of existing assumptions to recognize and exploit a killer app.

Q: How can a company or entrepreneur know if their technology radar is up to speed?

A: They need to focus on those digital technologies that are ready for inspection and experimentation. In particular, focus on innovations that don't seem to fit into existing market economics or are considered just not quite technically ready. The fact of the matter is that feasibility assumptions always lag behind true feasibility. Entrepreneurs should, therefore, spend time experimenting. To quote computer pioneer Gordon Bell, "A demo is worth a thousand pages of a business plan."

Q: Are there certain industries you see as being particularly ripe for killer apps to take hold?

A: It's actually harder to come up with industries that are not ripe for killer apps. Technology is transforming almost every industry faster than companies in those industries can respond. This lag between what's possible and how long it takes companies to respond creates the opening for killer apps.

Q: Can you give some examples of small companies in various industries that ignored the conventional wisdom, went up against industry leaders, and created killer apps in the process?

A: Internet access providers all over the world are examples of startups that played on the ignorance of telecommunications giants to provide corporations and consumers access to the Internet. Now these companies are reaping massive premiums as their larger competitors respond. Netscape, Amazon.com, Yahoo!, CD-Now, Edmunds, Auto-By-Tel, WebTV, and a host of other Web pioneers also went against industry leaders and are generating tremendous value for their founders and backers.

Q: What advice would you give younger people, specifically college students, on entrepreneurship and starting their own business?

A: My advice to first-time entrepreneurs is to overdo and underdo it at the same time. Overdo it on the sheer audacity of your idea; what to you is glaringly obvious couldn't be thought of by a large corporation's strategy group, no matter how many retreats they hold, consultants they hire, or focus groups they commission. In fact, these are precisely the reasons they can't do what you can do without really trying. Underdo it on the scale of your operation. Getting the big idea is not the hard part of succeeding with a startup; the difficulty is always in the operations. Accept the fact that you have no experience running a business, which does take skill and practice, and start small, work carefully, and watch for signs of trouble. Borrowing money you can't possibly repay? Falling behind in collections? Fighting with your partners all the time? These are the little things that sink big, smart ideas. To overcome them, set aside 25 percent of the time you spend on your venture to be completely realistic, serious, mature, and practical. During that time, admit to all of the small problems and minor difficulties that can add up to real trouble. Devise sensible solutions and act on them immediately. That still leaves 75 percent of the time to have fun. And over time, if you're really an entrepreneur, you'll come to enjoy the 25 percent as well. (Downes and Mui interview 1998)

Reprinted by permission of Harvard Business School Press, Boston, MA, 1998.

Incorporation

Information and Action Needed to Incorporate

1. What will be the corporation's name? _____

2. Who is the incorporator(s) and what is his or her address? _____

3. What type of corporation is being formed? _____

4. If an S corporation is being formed, an application for recognition of S status (form 2553) will have to be filed before the 16th day of the third month of the tax year in which the election is to take effect.

Application for Employer Identification Number

1 Will the corporation be employing anyone? If so, when is the first employee expected to be hired? _____

2. What is the corporation's fiscal year end? _____

3. What will be the corporation's principal activity? _____

4. Will the corporation be selling goods or services to the public (retail), to business (wholesale), or other? _____

5. Has the corporation previously applied for a federal employer identification number? If not, form SS-4 will have to be filed, either via mail or telephone call with fax. _____

6. What is the social security number of the officer who will be signing the SS-4? _____

Offices

1. Where will the main office be located? _____

2. Are there or will there be any branch offices? _____

3. Will you be doing business in more than one state? If so, which states? _____

Other Questions

1. Who are the advisory board members? _____

2. How many shareholders do you have, and who are they? _____

3. When do you hold shareholders' and directors' meetings? _____

Notes _____
_____
_____
_____
_____
_____
_____
_____

Tax Issues

What type of organization will your business be? (sole proprietorship, partnership, corporation, limited liability company, or other) _____

How will this affect the type and amount of taxes that you will pay? _____

What is the sales tax for the state or states in which you are conducting business and that you will be charging your customers? _____

If you have employees, what will be the amount withheld from employees' paychecks? _____

What payroll taxes is the company required to pay? _____

Should you consult with a tax specialist to determine the level of tax preparation you will need? _____

Are there any professors you can consult for tax advice? _____

Notes _____
_____
_____
_____
_____
_____
_____

Business Risks and Liabilities

In offering your product or service, what liability issues might you possibly face? _____
_____

Will your employees be handling heavy machinery or operating motor vehicles where they could be hurt?

How high a risk are external factors such as fire, theft, and vandalism? _____

Do you have clients sign a contract that frees your business from all external liabilities for which you are not at fault? _____

Have you incorporated your business to protect your personal assets? _____

Have you discussed with your partners standard operating procedures for major decisions to prevent one person from making decisions or taking actions that could harm the entire company? _____

What other risks and liabilities could your business be subject to? _____
_____
_____
_____
_____

Notes _____
_____
_____
_____
_____
_____
_____

Part IV

Quick Reference Guide

Building a Web Site

Sample Business Ideas

Entrepreneurial Resources Guide

Chapter 9

Building a Web Site

The World Wide Web

The World Wide Web has had a profound effect on small businesses throughout the world. Many college students use the World Wide Web and e-mail almost daily for both social and educational purposes. For the $70 to register your Web site and $10 to $15 a month to host your site, you can establish a presence where anyone with an Internet connection can learn about your business. Programs such as Microsoft Frontpage can even help you design your site. By setting up a Web page and being able to access e-mail, you are able to communicate with an international market.

The World Wide Web has the potential to be the most valuable marketing tool for your business, especially if you can sell your product over your site. You have the capability to establish a virtual store and process all orders from your dorm room. The shipping costs are a small price to pay for the ability to work out of your room instead of having to rent an office.

Creating a site for your collegiate businesses can be an important and worthwhile project. (Galani 1998)

Money and Time Constraints

The cost of your Web site will depend on several factors, such as how it is produced, how it is maintained, and how much you are benefiting financially as a result of your site. If you plan to do business on your site, it is worthwhile to put a good deal of funding into its creation and to hire a reputable Web design and programming firm.

The time you are willing to spend on your site affects the scope, rate of content turnover, and the general maintenance of the site. If you are conducting business or distributing information over your site, daily maintenance and check of your site is necessary to deal with any technical problems or user questions and feedback. Otherwise, maintenance is determined by necessity. Try not to let information get outdated, and never alienate your online clientele.

No matter what kind of site you build, you should include an e-mail link on all of your pages for user feedback. This will help you keep things working smoothly and is the best way to determine if you are reaching your desired audience.

Securing a Domain Name

The domain is the location of your site on the Internet, or the address, better known as the URL, or universal resource locator. Just as important as setting up a suitable Web site for your company is securing an appropriate domain name for your Web site. This is a step you should pursue even before the production of your site as domain names are grabbed up fast. Your business's Web address, following http://, will read: www.yourdomainname.com if you are a commercial business or www.yourdomainname.org if you are an organization.

It is a good idea to select a domain name that is the same as the name of your company. If that name is already taken, try to obtain the domain name for an acronym for your company or something related to the services you supply. To get a domain name, go to http://www.internic.net. Once you have registered and paid for your domain name, you can set up your account through a service provider.

Building a Web Page

According to Judy Galani, a Web-site developer for theknot.com in New York City, every business should have a Web site. It costs relatively little to put a simple Web page live on the Internet, so it is certainly an option you should consider for your collegiate business. However, for your Web site to benefit your company, it is important that the pages you create are clean, sharp, and to the point and that they serve to augment your business as much as possible.

Before going any further, you should take some time to research Web sites of companies similar to yours, as well as other sites on the Internet. Decide which designs appeal to you and which sites stand out from others. This will help you select the structure, look, and content of your site. Once the ideas begin springing up, you will be ready to start planning your own Web site. (Galani 1998)

Web-site Goals

Many times a Web site's only purpose is to serve as a digital advertisement for a company. The Web is perhaps the most cost effective form of advertising; it costs relatively little for upkeep yet can reach millions of people. But a Web site has the capability to serve many other varied functions, functions that are business savvy, educational, and fun. These other purposes include information distribution, commerce, community building, and entertainment.

Keep in mind, though, that the more complex a site is, the more time and money will be required for upkeep. Even if your business is a commerce-based business, the time and management constraints of conducting business over the Web may outweigh the benefits, and you might want to restrict your site to advertising and information distribution.

The goal of fulfilling the needs of your potential customers will shape the purpose, structure, and design of your Web site as well as of any other advertising, link exchange, and moneymaking ventures. It is important to know whom you are trying to reach to figure out the best way to attain that goal. In addition to knowing who your customers are and how you will reach them, it is equally important to consider where to reach them. Then you can buy advertising space, if your funds permit, or set up link exchanges on Web areas that would attract your potential clients. With so many people connected to the Internet today, your customers online are probably no different from the customers and clients you deal with offline. (Galani 1998)

Web-site Design

According to Ami Plasse, a Web designer for Blue Dingo Digital in New York City, good design is critical in the creation and operation of almost any business in college or anywhere else. For some businesses, the design should be simple yet intelligent in order to successfully and attractively organize and distribute the necessary information to the customer. For other businesses, especially ones that are more consumer oriented, a strong graphic look may be used to create recognition or familiarity with the company. In even others, a more highly developed design style or concept may be used for a company trying to convey a certain image. Whether you use the design for simple promotional and informational materials, print or broadcast advertising, online, or other types of interactive technology, a well executed and intelligent use of design is a crucial element in the success of your business.

Visual design in a Web site is slightly more complex than that of traditional media because of several key factors. One of the most important is bandwidth. Due to the limits of download times over regular phone lines, you must always keep in mind the file sizes of your pages and carefully consider the pros and cons of increasing file size to enhance the content of the site. Another factor is the partial loss of control that you have over the way your pages will be viewed. Depending on both a user's hardware and personal preferences, your page can be viewed through a variety of different browser applications, many of which can produce varying results for the same page. It can be stretched to a variety of shapes and sizes and viewed at different screen resolutions and color depths.

If your main objective is e-commerce, for instance, you most likely would want a fairly simple, straightforward visual design, which would allow the user to access information and view a product as quickly and easily as possible. For a site where the main objective is the entertainment of the user, a design allowing for larger file sizes would allow for the kind of content that is more rewarding for them. If you have a site that combines these objectives as well as possibly others, such as information distribution and retrieval, product branding, or community building, you may need to compromise on certain aspects.

If your target market are people in the 13 to 30 age group, you probably can use a more contemporary visual style. You can generally assume that this user has more up-to-date software versions and plug-ins and higher end hardware. This can allow you to use more complex and advanced visual technology and a more distinct visual style. If you are targeting middle to senior age users, you will generally have to be simpler and more straightforward in your design. You may want to use a more traditional visual style as well. If you are targeting all users, you may want a visual design that will appeal to the broadest group possible while keeping up a high enough level of sophistication to interest many types of individuals. (Plasse 1998)

Building Your Web Site

Once you have a clear idea of your site's purpose and resources, you can begin to create it. The most important thing to consider as you build your Web site is what will make it truly distinguishable. After you see your competitors' Web sites, you have an idea of what already exists. Most of the business content on the Web today is static and indistinguishable. Thus making your Web site stand out should be your main focus as you tackle the next steps towards finishing it. (Galani 1998)

Web-site Content

Once you know your objective, you can decide where to place all of the necessary content on your site. Depending on the amount of information you have, your content should be organized into sections, or even layers, of information. As long as your navigation paths remain clear, a layered organization will keep the body of your site from appearing jumbled. However, the structure should be set up in a way that you can make any necessary changes or add content without compromising your current design.

You should also think about user capability while working out the functionality. While building a Web site, it is easy to get carried away with new technologies, flashy animation, or eye-catching applets. But remember that it is not enough to know whom you want to reach; you also have to make sure that you can reach them. Shockwave movies and Flash animations require special plug-ins, while Java applets are not supported on all browsers. If you wish to include any of those multimedia, take time to provide alternative options for users who do not have the special plug-ins.

Finally, determine if you will require a database to return search results or forms to collect visitor information. If so, the basic structure of your Web site will be more complicated than you can construct using a basic authoring program. Databases and forms require common gateway interface (CGI) scripts. Your internet service provider (ISP) may have such scripts available for your use. If not, you will most likely need to consult and contract a programmer. (Galani 1998)

Web-site Production

When you have decided on the look and structure of your Web site, you can start putting everything together. If your budget allows, your best bet is to work with a Web design company that will provide the programming, graphic design, and writing for your site. If yours is a commerce-based site, you will definitely need the expertise of their entire staff to set up your Web pages. But if your site is simpler, your budget is small, and you are ambitious enough to produce the site yourself, you might need a crash course in Web-site authoring, graphic production, and file formats.

Unlike a printed work, a Web site is never technically finished. Changes can be made as often as you like. Therefore, maintenance is as important to your site as the initial construction itself. Consider how often changes will be necessary when planning the future maintenance of your site. If the maintenance will be handled by an outside source, set up a regular timetable for revisions. If changes will occur often, or irregularly, it might be less expensive to learn how to handle them yourself.

When production is complete and at last your pages are functional, all that is left is to transfer your company's Web page from the desktop to your server. This requires file transfer protocol (FTP), the process of uploading your text pages, graphics, and any other related files to your live server. To do this, you will need FTP software, which is standard on such programs as Microsoft Frontpage; your completed files, saved in the proper formats; an Internet connection; and a destination on a server. Once uploaded via FTP, your page will become live instantly. (Galani 1998)

Attracting Hits

As with any business, to get the word out about what you have to offer, you want to generate as many visits to your store or, in this case, as many hits on your Web site as possible. Hits are the number of times that people view each page of your Web site. Submitting your URL to search engines is only the first step. Another way to make your site available to searches is by including meta-list tags with any pertinent key words in your hypertext markup language (HTML) documents. This will call up your site on a search engine whenever that key word is typed. Search for existing Web rings, which are series of similar sites linked one to the next, that you might want to join. And, most importantly, include the URL of your site on any print or video materials produced by or for your company. (Galani 1998)

Find ways to market your business to attract users to your Web site. Include links to other interesting places on the Web. Many Web sites are now trading reciprocal links to each other's sites. Contact LinkExchange (www.linkexchange.com) to get started. Try to get links to your Web site from friends with their own personal Web pages and from other school-sponsored Web pages and businesses.

Now imagine that you have an office and you have clients or customers inside. What's the only foolproof way of keeping them inside? By locking the doors, of course. The same is true for your Web site. Though technically you may not be able to lock all paths out of your Web site, you can limit the number of possible exit paths. Don't include many links to other sites, or put them deep into a subsection of your site. Should you include links to pages outside of your site, program your pages to open any linked pages in a new and separate browser window. That way, your site remains open on the desktop. Most importantly, make the navigation easy to follow to avoid frustrating your viewer.

Attracting first-time visitors to your site is only the first step. When you hook your viewers the first time, you must quickly give them an incentive to return. Possible means of enticement include daily or weekly updates of interesting articles or information, promises of sales or new merchandise, and relationship-forming tools such as gathering a mailing list of potential customers or clients. (Galani 1998)

Web sites are a way for all companies, regardless of their size, to create a presence that allows customers to view their business. The World Wide Web can be one your most valuable tools in effectively marketing your business to your targeted customers at a low cost.

Chapter 10

Sample Business Ideas

Late-night Delivery Service

Late night on college campuses is arguably the busiest time of the day. Droves of students are out and about in search of some form of entertainment or relaxation, ultimately returning home hungry at a time when stores and restaurants are closed. Most business owners are not willing to stay open during these late hours, which leaves room for an enterprising individual to capitalize on the ignored and hungry late-night crowd. Set up a business that caters to the late-night college students. Create a delivery service with all sorts of food, desserts, and videos, either from existing stores on your college campus or from an inventory you stock yourself from local bulk-food stores. Put your menu on the World Wide Web and accept orders via e-mail or the phone. If you start the business with a couple of friends, you can take turns running the late-night shifts. Or consider being open only from Wednesday through Saturday. You can usually count on college students being hungry when they come home after partying and happy to buy from someone nearby.

Late-night Delivery Service

Notes _____

_____

_____

Possible Partners _____

Questions _____

_____

_____

Online Magazine

Create an online magazine with a list of current happenings at your school. Although there probably already exists a campus newspaper as well as other publications, you can offer fresh new content such as a gossip column, interviews with students on random topics, chat rooms, and other information that would not normally appear in other publications. Generate publicity for your online magazine by getting other students to participate by writing columns on a weekly basis. Then offer advertising services to local and national businesses that are interested in connecting with the college crowd. As ad rates in campus newspapers get increasingly expensive, you can offer these advertisers a new alternative. Make sure to keep the traffic on your site as high as possible because this is the information advertisers will use to determine their interest. Get some of your friends together who have experience building Web pages and create other niches to your site such as chat rooms and live discussion forums. This will give your Web site a truly different feel than the conservative newspaper and other publications that have been around since the university was founded.

Online Magazine

Notes _____

_____

_____

Possible Partners _____

Questions _____

_____

_____

Roommate-finder Service

When starting a roommate-finder service, the first thing to do is to set up a database of information on potential customers. Some of the questions you will have to ask include desired monthly rent, smoker versus nonsmoker, early riser versus night owl, girlfriend or boy friend sleepover status, degree of cleanliness, and type of person they are compatible with. The most affordable way to have your customers respond is through e-mail and a pager that has a voice mailbox. Decide how much to charge for the service and how you are going to collect payment. If you want to get upscale, you can even accept credit cards. Results can be sent to the client via traditional mail or e-mail. Next, create fliers and post them around campus and on nearby colleges. Besides marketing on kiosks, bulletin boards around campus, and in the campus newspaper, have your friends tell all their other friends. Also, get your friends to help by giving them referral bonuses for bringing in a new client. The key is to establish a large enough database to be able to successfully match up people with similar interests. Once you have an established database and are successful in matching roommates, your business will increase.

Roommate-finder Service

Notes _____

_____

_____

Possible Partners _____

Questions _____

_____

_____

T-shirt Business

T-shirts will be around for a long time because college students incorporate them into their daily wardrobe. To begin a T-shirt business, you must first establish what your fixed costs are going to be. If you have access to silk-screening materials and can produce the finished T-shirts yourself, the profit margin will be considerably higher. Otherwise, shop around to find the least inexpensive source of T-shirts and supply the shirts and the design to the printer in order to save an extra dollar or two per shirt. Next, decide what type of T-shirts to make. If you want to feature popular events, consider sports events, campus functions, sorority and fraternity activities, freshman orientation, parents' weekend, homecoming, and graduation. You can market your business by word of mouth and by placing fliers on kiosks and bulletin boards. Run special promotions to increase sales, such as "buy 10 T-shirts for your dorm and get one free." Try selling them during major campus events such as homecoming and football games, or go door to door in the dorms. Get a couple of friends together to put up some seed money to get the first round of T-shirts produced.

T-shirt Business

Notes _____

_____

_____

Possible Partners _____

Questions _____

_____

_____

Old Exam Files

Students are almost always nervous about how to prepare for exams. Reviewing old exams is often the best way to get a sense of what the tests are going to be like. Contact friends and professors to accumulate all of the exams they have available. Speak with your fraternity and sorority friends who may have access to their exam files to see if you can make copies of them. Then circulate fliers offering cash for old exams that other students around campus may have. Start a file of the different exams that you have accumulated for each class. Develop a Web page that advertises all of the different classes that you have exams for, then circulate fliers leading students to your Web site. Your service does not have to be solely exams; you can also provide study guides and notes for various classes. Also, list names of fellow students who have done exceptionally well in different classes and who would be willing to tutor others. Create the all-inclusive resource for students when it comes to exam time. You will be amazed at how much students are willing to pay for excellent study material.

Old Exam Files

Notes _____

_____

_____

Possible Partners _____

Questions _____

_____

_____

Spring Break Travel Packages

Taking a trip during spring break is a tradition for many college students. Go to your local travel agent and work out a deal for all of the spring-break travellers you bring into their agency. This can even result in a free trip for yourself and possibly a commission on each person you bring in. Whether you are short on cash and need extra money for your own spring break or just want to learn about the travel industry, this is a great opportunity to work as a liaison between the travel agents and the college community. Post fliers around campus and spread the word among your friends to start putting groups together for spring break. Most college students travel in groups on their spring break vacation, so there is a good opportunity to bring in several people at a time.

Spring Break Travel Packages

Notes _____

_____

_____

Possible Partners _____

Questions _____

_____

_____

Catering Service

There are events happening every day on college campuses that require catering. Although there may be existing catering services, hosts often look for new and innovative ways to have their party catered. Whether you offer an around-the-clock set-up and clean-up service or new and exciting cuisine that is currently not being offered, use your ingenuity to distinguish your catering service in the market-place. Decide what your advantage will be over your competitors, then send out letters to potential clients describing your service and the advantages your business offers. You can also work with existing catering companies to be a special service arm that they currently do not offer. Because special events are happening all over the campus and in the local community throughout the year, make sure you are informed about upcoming events by keeping in contact with the leaders of the sororities and fraternities, campus groups, and faculty.

Catering Service

Notes _____

_____

_____

Possible Partners _____
Questions _____

_____

_____

Tutoring Business

Tutoring is a win-win situation for all involved. You can become a tutor yourself or act as a manager, employing different students who performed well above average in various classes and splitting the profits of every tutoring session they hold. The first step is to assemble people who have done extremely well in specific core classes offered at your university and who also are good at working with others. Then, market your tutoring service to those currently enrolled in the class by obtaining the student enrollment lists for each of the classes you offer tutoring in. Check with the university administration to see if they will subsidize some of the students' tutoring costs. You may then be able to advertise your services through the university for free. Make sure to have extra tutors during midterm and finals. You may want to offer special group rates during these increased volume times to help spread the word about your business. If there already exists a university tutoring program, look for ways to differentiate your program, provide services they are lacking, or work in conjunction with them to offer more comprehensive services.

Tutoring Business

Notes _____

_____

_____

Possible Partners _____

Questions _____

_____

_____

Food Stands

College students will almost always eat large quantities of food at the most unlikely times of day. Find a way to provide quick and easy food to students between their classes, then get people to run your stands at various high-traffic points throughout campus. By offering items such as fresh fruit, sandwiches, snacks, and other ready-made items, you will be able to provide quick power-up snacks to hungry students passing by. Make sure to contact the city for vending certification and licenses and also to look into city or state food handling regulations or restrictions. Try to work with the university to accept their meal cards in lieu of cash payments. As college campuses continue to move further away from using cash, the businesses that are debit and credit card friendly will be the ones with increased sales.

Food Stands

Notes _____

_____

_____

Possible Partners _____

Questions _____

_____

_____

Recycling Service

If you live in a state where you can collect a return on cans and bottles, you have an opportunity to make some extra cash in a hurry. The return on recycling may not seem like much for one can, but it adds up quickly. The best time to collect recyclables is after large parties across campus when empty cans and bottles are thrown everywhere.

Or before a big party, make a deal with the host or hostess to set up a partnership on the profits from the recyclables. Another way is to work with the university to set up recycling bins around campus. Strike a deal with the university to make it mutually beneficial for both sides to start a recycling initiative that includes all types of recyclables. Recycling is another win-win proposition for all involved.

Recycling Service

Notes _____

_____

_____

Possible Partners _____

Questions _____

_____

_____

Tapestry and Poster Sales

College students love to have their walls covered with eclectic art. Tapestries are a fun and effective way to cover a lot of wall space, and the other great wall fillers are posters and prints. Most tapestries that cost about $20 originate from some place abroad such as India for less than $1. There exists an outstanding opportunity to try your hand at being the middlemarket supplier between the college student and the importer. Once you have located a supplier via the Internet or local dealers, try selling tapestries door to door in the dorms and in other on-campus living places. This is especially successful the first week or two of the semesters when students are still trying to find anything to cover their walls. Or set up a kiosk outside the student center, but make sure to clear it with the university first. Get a couple of friends together and plaster the campus with signs for your poster and tapestry sale. Then follow up after the sale with door-to-door sales to catch the impulse buyers who would normally not purchase them at the bookstore.

Tapestry and Poster Sales

Notes _____

_____

Possible Partners _____

Questions _____

_____

_____

Coffeehouse

Most college students love to hang out and relax over a cup of coffee, whether listening to music, smoking cigarettes and cigars, or just talking with friends. Create a place where college students can congregate and relax, get something to eat, and enjoy a little entertainment. You might rent out a space on your college campus on a part-time basis or open up your own off-campus apartment one or two nights a week. Make up a menu of sandwiches, beverages, and dessert; get some friends who play musical instruments and turn your place into a swinging coffeehouse. Either collect a cover charge at the door or just make your money off the food and drinks sold over the course of the evening. Get your roommates together and see how they feel about turning your apartment into a coffeehouse occasionally for some extra cash.

Coffeehouse

Notes _____

_____

_____

Possible Partners _____

Questions _____

_____

_____

Discount Coupons on the Internet

Students are always looking for a bargain. Whether it is free meals or discounts on clothing and compact discs, people love to get a good deal. Work with local merchants and restaurant owners to put together a Web site of coupons to offer to college students at your campus. Put the coupons online and allow students to print them out, avoiding any printing costs of your own. The key is to get advertisements in the hands of the target market. Work out a deal with the advertisers whereby you get paid on each advertisement made or by each sale your advertisement generates. By serving as a liaison between local business owners and the student body, you can capitalize on your inside knowledge of the types of advertisements and special promotions that will appeal to students and thus generate additional revenue for your advertisers.

Discount Coupons on the Internet

Notes _____

_____

_____

Possible Partners _____

Questions _____

_____

_____

Collegiate Marketing Service

Many companies would like to market their product or service to college students. However, it is often difficult for them to accurately gauge what college students are currently interested in and how best to market their products to them. Large companies are often willing to pay well to get their name spread across college campuses. Companies like Gillette, Mountain Dew, AT&T, Sprint, MCI, and various magazines and newspapers actively market to college students nationwide. Set up a service that helps these or other companies effectively cater to college students. Whether it is putting up fliers across campus, setting up stands on local walkways, or just spreading the word with the help of your friends, your service will be an invaluable resource to the company you are representing. Look around your campus to see what products or services currently exist, and then determine what other products and services would also excel. Once you have decided how you will help these companies, send letters to the people in their marketing department and check out their Web pages for possible contacts. Convince these companies that with your help they will soon have a commanding presence on your college campus.

Collegiate Marketing Service

Notes _____

_____

_____

Possible Partners _____

Questions _____

_____

_____

Wake-up Service

Have you ever slept through an important class, event, or even a final exam? College students in particular have trouble waking up due to late nights or their roommate tripping over the alarm clock in the middle of the night. A good number of students will be more than willing to pay a couple of extra dollars a week or month to ensure that they wake up for classes and exams. Advertise your wake-up service with fliers around your campus and nearby colleges. Set up a Web page where students can sign up online. You can offer options to call them at home, on their cellular phone, pager, or even via e-mail. You can even have your business operate only around exam time. Or you can market your business as a year-round reminder service of important upcoming events. Try offering your service in 5- and 10-call packages over the course of a month. Once you have them hooked, they will keep coming back to assure that they will not oversleep or miss an important event.

Wake-up Service

Notes _____

_____

_____

Possible Partners _____

Questions _____

_____

_____

Video Delivery Service

Most college students love movies. With the cost of movie tickets rising annually, videos will undoubtedly continue to increase in popularity. You can now buy a video for the cost of a couple of movie tickets. You might either pool money and purchase videos with your friends or work with an existing video store to deliver their movies and help them increase their business on your campus. Contact the area movie distributor to find out the rules and rates involved with renting movies. Since most college students have access to e-mail and the Web in their room or nearby, list your movies online and allow them to order a movie via e-mail that you will deliver to their door at an arranged time. If you are working out of your apartment, make a deal with an existing business location to set up a drop box where the movies can be returned. You need not limit yourself to just renting movies, however. Lots of money can be made by offering snacks, desserts, and beverages to be delivered with the movies.

Video Delivery Service

Notes _____

_____

_____

Possible Partners _____

Questions _____

_____

_____

Product Marketing Service

Are there products and services that exist on your college campus that you think would be successful in other parts of the country or on other college campuses? All highly successful companies must start somewhere, and it is often with a small storefront or in a local town. If you have a good sense of what will be successful, make a list of businesses that you are familiar with and companies that you think have a novel concept or idea. Learn everything you can about these businesses and whether they are marketing in other parts of the country. Put together a presentation to give to the owners of the business showing them how they could be even more successful by expanding to other areas or college campuses. Offer to lead up the initiative to generate additional revenue by working with your friends at other schools and with job placement offices at other campuses.

Product Marketing Service

Notes _____

_____

_____

Possible Partners _____

Questions _____

_____

_____

Vending Machine and Arcade Unit Business

Quarters and dimes can add up to a lot of money in the vending business. Vending machines and arcade units are a great way to make money with little up-front investment. Most vending companies will help you finance the cost of the unit over a set amount of time and make it feasible for you to still make money. Think about where there is a lot of traffic flow at your college. Work out a deal with the manager of a highly trafficked location to split profits from your vending unit. As you make more and more money, invest in other units to place around the campus and begin to build your vending business while making contacts with the business community at your college.

Vending Machine and Arcade Unit Business

Notes _____

_____

Possible Partners _____

Questions _____

_____

_____

Tuxedo Rental Service

Most college students do not own tuxedos, yet there are many social events on campus that require formal attire. Work with an existing tuxedo rental store to get a portion of the rental fees for each person you bring in. Market the company's tuxedos to fraternities, campus groups, and sports teams that have black-tie events throughout the year. You could also try to form a partnership with your local dry cleaner and convince them of the lucrative possibilities of tuxedo rental. Most tuxedo stores are not on university campuses, so having any sort of presence at a college university would be a real benefit to them.

Tuxedo Rental Service

Notes _____

_____

Possible Partners _____

Questions _____

_____

_____

Internet Marketing Service

The Internet continues to grow in popularity every day. College students now use the World Wide Web and e-mail daily for their classes as well as their entertainment. They surf the Web for hours at a time and use e-mail to keep in touch with friends and loved ones almost as much as they use the phone. The World Wide Web provides the perfect link between college students and businesses. Find businesses with a product or service that you feel would be in great demand by college students at your university, then work with these businesses to show them what appeals to college students and how to market to them effectively using the Internet and e-mail. If you help them market their product or service successfully to other college students, you'll become a necessary and vital bridge between the business world and college campuses.

Internet Marketing Service

Notes _____

_____

_____

Possible Partners _____

Questions _____

_____

_____

Tailgate Party Business

Tailgate parties are a popular way to socialize before football games and other university events. Students will linger for hours before and after the event, hanging out at these gatherings with their friends. This is a great time to start up your grill and throw on some hamburgers, hot dogs, and pretzels. The great smell of the barbecue should be all it takes to have customers heading your way. Because food inside the stadium is usually so expensive, you can afford to charge anywhere between two to four dollars for your hamburgers and one to two dollars for your hot dogs and pretzels. Chip in with a couple of your friends and make a trip to the supermarket to load up on the essentials for grilling. Mark your spot in the parking area and try to position yourself there every game day. While you have a captive audience at your grill, you may even want to try selling some other items such as T-shirts, hats, and mugs. Campus events such as football games can attract a huge number of people, so take advantage of this captive audience. This can be an easy way to earn money to pay for your ticket to the game in addition to some extra spending money for the weekend.

Tailgate Party Business

Notes _____

_____

_____

Possible Partners _____

Questions _____

_____

_____

Alumni Address Guide

While you are still in college, you know exactly how to get in touch with your classmates. As you get closer to graduation, you realize that everyone is going their separate ways and there will be a lot of people you may never see again. Although the university holds alumni weekends and has magazines that explain what a select few former students are currently doing, most universities do not have detailed alumni record keeping guides. This may be a good project to undertake with your university's help. When you are still in college is the perfect time to start planning for the release of your guide book. The key is to find out from the graduating class where they will be next year and to get their new address, phone number, and e-mail address. The difficulty is obtaining the necessary information from as many individuals as possible in a timely manner. After compiling your data, you will have an entire database of people to market your book to. Promote it as an excellent way for people to contact friends from school and also to make business contacts. You can even come up with updated versions in the years to follow.

Alumni Address Guide

Notes _____

_____

Possible Partners _____

Questions _____

_____

_____

Tanning Salon

A good number of college students are always looking to improve their tan. It does not take much space or many beds to be able to open your own tanning salon. Finding a small retail space and ordering a couple of tanning beds should cost about $2,000 or $3,000. If this is too much money, find some of your friends who may want to chip in. Do your research to make sure there are no nearby tanning salons that currently exist. Tanning beds do not take up much room, so you will only need a small space to put them in. Try to find a location that is within walking distance for most students. The best way to market your business will be to put up fliers around campus. Offer special promotions, gift certificates, and group packages, then spread the word that your campus now has a tanning salon.

Tanning Salon

Notes _____

_____

_____

Possible Partners _____

Questions _____

_____

_____

Graphic Design Business

Many small or newly formed organizations cannot afford to hire professionals to produce their graphics. Having an eye for good design, a creative mind, and access to a computer and printer will enable you to establish a business helping individuals, groups, and organizations better reach their customers with effective graphic design. You can offer to design their logo, advertisements, fliers, letterhead, and even Web pages. Potential clients may include local businesses, student groups, athletic teams, and university officials who sponsor campus activities. Market your business with fliers around campus and in the neighboring areas. Make sure to spend time making your advertisements look professional and unique. Enlist other students with creative talent to help you design different samples for potential clients. Once you have an established client list, you can begin branching out to offer other services as well.

Graphic Design Business

Notes _____

_____

Possible Partners _____

Questions _____

_____

_____

Care Package Service

Most parents love to send their children care packages as little reminders that they are thinking of them. Create a business in which you assemble and mail or deliver these care packages for them. Go to your local bulk food store and make a list of items that would interest college students. Give parents the option of choosing which type of items they send to their children, such as a healthy care package, a pick-me-up care package, a congratulations care package, a holiday care package, and others. Either put together a mailer of your own or try to work with the university to place an advertisement on a piece of mail they send to parents. A good time to advertise directly to parents is during parents' weekend and when students move in to their living units at the beginning of the year. Care packages are a great way to make both parents and students happy.

Care Package Service

Notes _____

_____

_____

Possible Partners _____

Questions _____

_____

_____

Ride Service

There are always students looking for a way to get to the airport, downtown, or to a big event off campus. By establishing a shuttle service, you can cater to their needs and make a handsome profit. Take the necessary steps to insure yourself and your business. There can be a lot of liability involved with being responsible for driving other individuals, yet you probably can insure your business for less than $100 a month. One way to avoid this expense would be to work with an existing taxi or shuttle business. Form a partnership in which you get a commission for each customer you bring to them. Take care of all the marketing needs on campus and promote the business through your friends and word-of-mouth advertising. By establishing a relationship with an existing business, you shed most of the liability and can still make money by bringing them customers.

Ride Service

Notes _____

_____

_____

Possible Partners _____

Questions _____

_____

_____

Online Gift-giving Service

Set up a Web site that allows students, parents, and friends to send gifts to their loved ones at the click of a button. There are always parties, holidays, and special events going on at college campuses across the nation for which people may want to send a gift, a card, or just a simple reminder that they are thinking of them. Events such as birthdays and holidays are times when parents usually send their child a gift of some sort. While parents represent one potential source of business, your fellow students represent another. By offering affordable gift packages that can be delivered to students on special days such as Valentine's Day, formals, and the traditional holidays, you will increase your target market. Try to get the university to place a link on their Web site to yours in return for a profit on each sale generated. Also try to obtain links on Web sites for campus groups and sports teams. By serving as a one-stop Web site for both parents' and students' gift-giving needs, you will make it easier for them to send gifts to one another. With a virtual storefront, all you have to do is fill the orders and keep your Web site up-to-date.

Online Gift-giving Service

Notes _____

_____

_____

Possible Partners _____

Questions _____

_____

_____

_____

Party Place

It is no secret that parties are a large part of most college students' lives. After a couple of years of the same campus and fraternity gatherings, students start to look elsewhere for different types of events to attend. Check into renting out a space either on your campus or at a nearby location. Work out an arrangement with the owner to rent the space for the evening. Have them provide the drinks sold at the bar and handle the carding at the door, clean up, and liability coverage for any damages incurred. You will be responsible for marketing the event around campus and gathering a big group of people to attend the party, as well as possibly helping with the clean up duty. Collect a cover charge at the door and use these proceeds to pay for renting the space. Any money left over after the marketing and rental fee is straight profit for you. The bar or restaurant owner also benefits because of the fee for renting the space and the profits from drinks sold at the bar.

Party Place

Notes _____

_____

_____

Possible Partners _____

Questions _____

_____

_____

_____

Debit Card Service

With campus crime being a serious problem at numerous colleges, creating a cashless environment can make life safer for students. Many college campuses across the nation are trying to eliminate the need for students to carry around much cash. This is being done primarily through the use of debit cards, which are similar to credit cards but which make deductions from a revenue account or else tally an account with the bills sent directly to students' parents. Most colleges are employing and encouraging debit card use at dining halls, the campus bookstore, and other university-sponsored stores. However, there are still the local restaurants and stores that are not participating in this program. Work with them to establish a program whereby you create a network and a card for the students to use at their restaurants in return for a small percentage of every transaction. You handle the marketing and billing of the students and parents and provide them with the hardware necessary to conduct the transactions. This idea takes a bit of research but is a very valuable concept that will probably take hold more and more around college campuses nationwide in the near future.

Debit Card Service

Notes _____

_____

_____

Possible Partners _____

Questions _____

_____

_____

Collegiate Finances Assistance

Managing money in college is a very difficult task. Depending on the money a student receives from parents or jobs, there is seldom enough to cover loan payments, food, clothes, and entertainment, and still leave any spending money. Most students are having their first experience with managing their own money and find it difficult to watch what they spend yet are not ready for the advanced financial software that is on the market. One solution is for you to create a simple software program or spreadsheet book that helps college students chart their finances. By coming up with an easy way to track their money and with categories specifically designed to reflect a college student's expenses, income, and lifestyle, you will help them manage their money more effectively. You can market your book or software in college bookstores or get your own Web page and market it to colleges across the country.

Collegiate Finances Assistance

Notes _____

_____

_____

Possible Partners _____

Questions _____

_____

_____

_____

Coursework Hotline

Every student has difficulty from time to time in a certain class. Professors hold office hours only at certain times of the week, so if students need a question answered immediately, they might not get the help they need. You can provide one solution by means of a coursework hotline. Compile a list of students who have excelled in certain core classes at your university. Then set up a toll-free telephone number or online address area where students can call in or use instant messenger to get their questions answered. They can choose which class they need help in and pay by credit card. Offer your services in the evenings and especially around exam time. Try to form a relationship with some of the professors of the core classes you are offering services in. They may even provide you with some material to help answer specific questions or may supply their old exams. Market your phone number and Web site address on bulletin boards and kiosks at school, especially in the academic buildings. Focus first on specific core classes taken at your school. As your service becomes more popular, you can expand to offer your service for additional class subjects.

Coursework Hotline

Notes _____

_____

Possible Partners _____

Questions _____

_____

_____

Used Clothing Sales

While the grunge scene is nearly over, many college students still enjoy dressing in worn clothing that is different from the traditional Gap, Abercrombie & Fitch, or J. Crew styles. Try going to flea markets in your area or posting signs on campus to buy jeans and other articles of clothing that people do not wear any more. Most people who are getting rid of old clothes will be happy to get any small amount of money for them. Mark them up 50 to 100 percent over what you paid for them and resell them. In fact, items such as used jeans can often be sold at more than their original price. If you like dealing with clothes and have some space for storing and sorting, your recycled clothing business can be a real benefit to your customers. And if you like wearing used clothes, the advantage to you is getting first choice of the best items.

Used Clothing Sales

Notes _____

_____

_____

Possible Partners _____

Questions _____

_____

_____

Carpet Sales

Lots of college students would love to carpet their rooms and apartments but often can't find small amounts of carpeting that are affordable. Traditional carpet stores usually carry only the expensive top-of-the-line carpeting which they sell in large square-foot amounts. Make your niche in the market by either working with the established carpeting stores or buying left-over swatches of their carpet to resell. Go to the carpet stores and buy swatches that they have left over from previous projects. Get a rental truck, pile in all of the carpet, and sell the pieces outside of the dorms and apartment buildings. If you do not have the cash to buy all of the carpet from the store, try for an arrangement in which you get a percentage of every piece of carpet you sell. There are numerous ways to set up a carpet business because there is no established middle market.

Carpet Sales

Notes _____

_____

_____

Possible Partners _____

Questions _____

_____

_____

Laundry Service

Doing laundry in college is a task most college students would definitely like to avoid. Unfortunately, sending everything to a commercial dry cleaners gets extremely expensive. Even doing their own laundry at a laundromat will typically cost $4 to $6, plus the time and energy spent. You can offer an affordable alternative to your fellow students. Establish a laundry service that will even pick up and drop off their laundry. Allow students to arrange for service via your Web site, and inform them when it is done via e-mail. Get some extra students to help with the marketing and the laundry tasks. Charge by the pound, and offer special monthly and semester rates. By investing in your own machines, buying some second hand, or working with a local laundromat, you can create a nice profit for yourself.

Laundry Service

Notes _____

_____

_____

Possible Partners _____

Questions _____

_____

_____

Loft-building Service

In the cramped space of college dorm rooms, sometimes the only way to get some extra room is to build a loft. Lofts can be rather expensive and require quite a bit of knowledge on how to set them up, yet people are often willing to spend quite a bit of money to free up some space. Spend some time over the summer learning how to build lofts, and assemble a team of workers who can install them when school starts. Get to school before classes begin and advertise your services throughout the dorms and in other living areas. As orders come in, send your team of workers out to install the lofts. Be prepared before the orders come in so that you can respond in the most timely fashion and set up as many as possible.

Loft-building Service

Notes _____
_____
_____

Possible Partners _____
Questions _____
_____
_____
_____

Flea Market

Most college students are known for collecting mass amounts of clothing, furniture, compact discs, and a plethora of other stuff. They end up moving at the end of every year and are forced to relocate all of their belongings to another residence. They are often ready to get rid of some of their possessions to make room for new items. A flea market offers a setting where students can sell some of their old belongings and even pick up some new ones. You could even set up your flea market online if you have a place to store the items. By scanning pictures of the items onto your Web page, you give customers an idea of the product, and if they are interested in it, they can even bid on the item. There are many ways to set up a flea market, whether online or in a parking lot on campus so that you can take advantage of the multitude of belongings that college students accumulate throughout their years at college.

Flea Market

Notes _____

_____

_____

Possible Partners _____

Questions _____

_____

_____

Online Note-taking Center

Because it can be very difficult to make it to every class throughout the semester, there are usually notes that students wish they had from a missed class or two. You can fill the need by setting up a note-taking center online. Determine which are the core lecture classes that the greatest number of students attend. Get a group of intelligent and reliable students together who will go to every class and take copious notes, then market your class notes on a semester- and individual-class basis. You can even offer special extras, such as answers to previous exam questions or tutoring sessions with students who excelled in that class. Also set up chat rooms on your site for the different classes where students can exchange thoughts and questions with each other on a given subject. Market your service around campus and establish a home page on the Web where students can receive the notes via e-mail.

Online Note-taking Center

Notes _____

_____

_____

Possible Partners _____

Questions _____

_____

_____

Your Business Ideas

Type of business _____

Details _____

_____

_____

Notes _____

_____

_____

Possible partners _____

_____

Questions _____

_____

_____

Type of business _____

Details _____

_____

_____

Notes _____

_____

_____

Possible partners _____

_____

Questions _____

_____

_____

Type of business _____

Details _____

_____

_____

Notes _____

_____

_____

Possible partners _____

_____

Questions _____

_____

_____

Chapter 11

Entrepreneurial Resources Guide

Toll-free Telephone Number

You can get a toll-free number from most of the major long-distance telephone companies, including AT&T, MCI, Sprint, and others. Make sure to find the one that offers you the best rate for the number and cost per minute of incoming calls. This can get quite expensive, anywhere from 25 to 50 cents a minute on incoming calls, so make sure it is a worthwhile expense for your business.

Credit Card Capability

If you decide that you want your customers to be able to pay for your business's products or services with their credit card, the best place to look for credit card, or merchant banking, capabilities is either at your bank's local branch or online. There are also a number of businesses such as Costco that will provide this for your business. Merchant banking companies generally charge from one to three percent on every sale, depending on the type of business and volume of transactions. Do an online search for merchant banking to see the plethora of options available to your business.

Tax Forms

If you incorporate your business, usually the lawyer or incorporating agent will provide you with the proper tax forms for your business. If you have specific questions, try logging into a chat room on a tax Web site or Web sites for Entrepreneur Magazine or American Express Small Business. If you are a sole proprietor, your business's profit or loss will be part of your personal tax situation. You can get personal tax forms at the post office or city library early in the year.

Business Bank Accounts

Business bank accounts can be set up at almost any bank. It is a good idea to go to a bank that you are familiar with and where you have your personal account. The better relations you create now, the easier it will be to establish a line of credit or take out a loan in the future. Usually, if you can keep a balance of at least $2,000, most monthly maintenance fees will be waived.

Cellular Capabilities

The advantage of a cellular phone is that you can conduct sales while travelling. Most charge you air time only on incoming calls as long as you are in your zone, and hopefully most incoming calls will be sales. You can also get a voice mailbox on your phone, which is a great way to keep in touch with prospective customers. There are programs through AT&T and Nextel that offer one rate for making long distances and local calls. For around $85 dollars a month, you can get up to 500 free minutes, a voice mailbox, and the ability to receive e-mail on your phone.

Voice Mailboxes

If you do want phone calls coming through on your personal phone line, check into the option of a voice mailbox. Look in the Yellow Pages or on the Web at www.jfax.com It generally costs from $10 to $15 a month to have a dedicated phone number for your business. Services such as www.efax.com now even offer a free fax number over the Internet.

E-mail Addresses

Entrepreneurial Consulting

EPS Business Partners (www.epsbp.com)
SCORE (www.sba.gov)

Financing Information

Small Business Administration (www.sba.gov)
America's Business Funding Directory (www.businessfinance.com)
Vfinance.com (www.vfinance.com)
The Capital Network (www.thecapitalnetwork.com)
garage.com (www.garage.com)
FinanceHub (www.financehub.com)
MoneyHunter (www.moneyhunter.com)
Capital Venture (www.capitalventure.com)

Free E-mail Accounts

Hotmail (www.hotmail.com)
Yahoo! (www.yahoo.com)
Excite (www.excite.com)
Lycos (www.lycosemail.com)
Entrepreneur Magazine Online (www.entrepreneurmag.com)

Free Personal Web Pages

theglobe.com (www.theglobe.com)
GeoCities (www.geocities.com)
Tripod (www.tripod.com)
Inc. Magazine (www.inc.com)

General Publications

EntreWorld (www.entreworld.com)
Inc. Magazine (www.inc.com)
Entrepreneur Magazine (www.entrepreneurmag.com)
Silicon Alley Reporter (www.siliconalleyreporter.com)
Business Resource Center (www.morebusiness.com)
Entrepreneurial Edge (www.edgeonline.com)

General Publications (continued)

Fast Company (www.fastcompany.com)
Red Herring (www.herring.com)
Upside (www.upside.com)

Incorporating Information

Harvard Business Services (www.delawareinc.com)
The Company Corporation (www.incorporate.com)

Online Marketing Information

Guerrilla Marketing (www.gmarketing.com)
Register-It! (www.registerit.com)
AtWeb (www.atweb.com)
SubmitIt! (www.submit.com)
LinkExchange (www.linkexchange.com)
NetCreations (www.netcreations.com)

References

Downes, Larry, and Chunka Mui. 1998. Press materials provided by Harvard Business School Press, Boston, MA.

Galani, Judy. 1998. Interview by author. 9 July.

Kleiman, Jonathan. 1998. Interview by author. 8 October.

Pierce, J. Corey. 1998. The raining money workbook. Corona, CA. Duplicated.

Plasse, Ami. 1998. Interview by author. 9 July.

Rappoport, Josh. 1998. Interview by author. 21 June.

Index

From The Leading Publisher of Small Business Information
Books that save you time and money.

This all-in-one, easy-to-understand guide will help you get started on the right foot. Packed with valuable start-up information, SmartStart Your (State) Business will prepare you to deal with federal, state, and local regulations imposed on small businesses. This concise, friendly, and up-to-date sourcebook is an affordable investment that details each critical step of starting your own business — from choosing a business structure to writing a top-notch business plan.

SmartStart Your (State) Series   **Approx. pages: 325**
Paperback: $19.95   **ISBN: different for each state**

Two very practical small business books in one. Book one offers competitive strategies and offers a number of defensive business models that can be adopted, copied, or modified to fit a particular business challenge. Book two, contains fourteen strategies that guarantee sales and profits. Each model contains a competitive strategy that will lessen the impact of a competitor's action by helping target and highly satisfy one specific type of customer.

Navigating the Marketplace   **Pages: 350**
Paperback: $21.95   **ISBN: 1-55571-458-7**

"Advertising," says author Kathy Kobliski, "is not a perfect science. It's not even close." For many small business owners, that means the potential for wasting thousands of dollars on the wrong advertising decisions. This guide is an ideal primer on the in's and out's of advertising and how to get the information you need to pinpoint your advertising objectives. Complete with worksheets, plus help in grasping the lingo, and techniques to target your defined market with the best medium.

Advertising Without An Agency   **Pages: 175**
Paperback: $19.95   **ISBN: 1-55571-429-3**

Surviving Success presents a program for those who wish to lead their companies from promising startup to industry dominance. Meet the challenges of business growth and transition with new insights. Learn from success stories. Be prepared to take proactive steps into your company's next growth transition.

Surviving Success   **Pages: 230**
Paperback: $19.95   **ISBN: 1-55571-446-3**

From The Leading Publisher of Small Business Information
Books that save you time and money.

Pursuing a high-tech business has never been more opportune, however the competition in the industry is downright grueling. Author Richard Manweller brings a smart, in-depth strategy with motivational meaning. It will show you how to tailor your strategy to grain investor's attention. If you are looking for a financial angel, Funding High-Tech Ventures is the guidance you need to make the right match.

Funding High-Tech Ventures   **Pages: 160**
Paperback: $21.95   **ISBN: 1-55571-405-6**

Learn how to position your products correctly in the international marketplace and how to begin the process of exploring sales avenues outside of the United States. Stresses the practical key differences of selling to foreign markets; how to find the all-important local marketing agents; covers required product and label changes; and gives advice on handling requests for under-the-table payoffs. Real-life example are highlighted throughout.

Developing International Markets   **Pages: 350**
Paperback: $21.95   **ISBN: 1-55571-433-1**

Connecting Online cuts through the hype and shows you why it is essential to first establish a solid image and communicative environment with your key audiences on the Internet. Through the authors' own personal experiences with the Internet, public relations, and the media, you will be able to skip the starry-eyed mistakes that many people make — and build a lasting and effective Internet strategy and presence. Examines all of the Internet tools (not just the World Wide Web) that can help you.

Connecting Online   **Pages: 475**
Paperback: $21.95   **ISBN: 1-55571-403-X**

This CD-ROM nicely integrates with your version of Microsoft Office and includes; Excel templates that will compute Profit and Loss, Cash Flow, Market and Sales Forecasting; Word business templates and five example business plans; A PowerPoint presentation example; and other files, templates and business helpers that will give you a professional edge when building a business plan.

Winning Business Plans in Color   **Windows MS-Office Addition**
Call for current pricing   CD-ROM

ALL MAJOR CREDIT CARDS ACCEPTED

| CALL TO PLACE AN ORDER
— or —
TO RECEIVE A FREE CATALOG | **1-800-228-2275** |

International Orders (541) 479-9464   *Fax Orders* (541) 476-1479
Web site http://www.psi-research.com   *Email* sales@psi-research.com

PSI Research   P.O. Box 3727   Central Point, Oregon   97502   U.S.A.

HOW TO ORDER

Mail:	Send this completed order form and a check, money order or credit card information to: **PSI Research/The Oasis Press®, P.O. Box 3727, Central Point, Oregon 97502-0032**
Fax:	Available 24 hours a day, 7 days a week at **1-541-476-1479**
Email:	info@psi-research.com (Please include a phone number, should we need to contact you.)
Web:	Purchase any of our products online at our Website at **http://www.psi-research.com/oasis.htm**

Inquiries and International Orders: Please call 1-541-479-9464

Indicate the quantity and price of the titles you would like: 5/99

TITLE	ISBN	BINDER	PAPERBACK	QTY.	TOTAL
Advertising Without An Agency	1-55571-429-3		☐ 19.95		
Before You Go Into Business Read This	1-55571-481-1		☐ 17.95		
Bottom Line Basics	1-55571-329-7 (B) ▪ 1-55571-330-0 (P)	☐ 39.95	☐ 19.95		
BusinessBasics	1-55571-430-7		☐ 16.95		
The Business Environmental Handbook	1-55571-304-1 (B) ▪ 1-55571-163-4 (P)	☐ 39.95	☐ 19.95		
Business Owner's Guide to Accounting and Bookkeeping	1-55571-381-5		☐ 19.95		
businessplan.com	1-55571-455-2		☐ 19.95		
Buyer's Guide to Business Insurance	1-55571-310-6 (B) ▪ 1-55571-162-6 (P)	☐ 39.95	☐ 19.95		
California Corporation Formation Package	1-55571-368-8 (B) ▪ 1-55571-464-1 (P)	☐ 39.95	☐ 29.95		
Collection Techniques for a Small Business	1-55571-312-2 (B) ▪ 1-55571-171-5 (P)	☐ 39.95	☐ 19.95		
College Entrepreneur Handbook	1-55571-503-6		☐ 16.95		
A Company Policy & Personnel Workbook	1-55571-364-5 (B) ▪ 1-55571-486-2 (P)	☐ 49.95	☐ 29.95		
Company Relocation Handbook	1-55571-091-3 (B) ▪ 1-55571-092-1 (P)	☐ 39.95	☐ 19.95		
CompControl	1-55571-356-4 (B) ▪ 1-55571-355-6 (P)	☐ 39.95	☐ 19.95		
Complete Book of Business Forms	1-55571-107-3		☐ 19.95		
Connecting Online	1-55571-403-X		☐ 21.95		
Customer Engineering	1-55571-360-2 (B) ▪ 1-55571-359-9 (P)	☐ 39.95	☐ 19.95		
Develop and Market Your Creative Ideas	1-55571-383-1		☐ 15.95		
Developing International Markets	1-55571-433-1		☐ 19.95		
Doing Business in Russia	1-55571-375-0		☐ 19.95		
Draw the Line	1-55571-370-X		☐ 17.95		
The Essential Corporation Handbook	1-55571-342-4		☐ 21.95		
Essential Limited Liability Company Handbook	1-55571-362-9 (B) ▪ 1-55571-361-0 (P)	☐ 39.95	☐ 21.95		
Export Now	1-55571-192-8 (B) ▪ 1-55571-167-7 (P)	☐ 39.95	☐ 24.95		
Financial Decisionmaking	1-55571-435-8		☐ 19.95		
Financial Management Techniques	1-55571-116-2 (B) ▪ 1-55571-124-3 (P)	☐ 39.95	☐ 19.95		
Financing Your Small Business	1-55571-160-X		☐ 19.95		
Franchise Bible	1-55571-366-1 (B) ▪ 1-55571-367-X (P)	☐ 39.95	☐ 24.95		
The Franchise Redbook	1-55571-484-6		☐ 34.95		
Friendship Marketing	1-55571-399-8		☐ 18.95		
Funding High-Tech Ventures	1-55571-405-6		☐ 21.95		
Home Business Made Easy	1-55571-428-5		☐ 19.95		
Improving Staff Productivity	1-55571-456-0		☐ 16.95		
Information Breakthrough	1-55571-413-7		☐ 22.95		
Insider's Guide to Small Business Loans	1-55571-488-9		☐ 19.95		
InstaCorp™ Book & Software	1-55571-382-3		☐ 29.95		
Joysticks, Blinking Lights, and Thrills	1-55571-401-3		☐ 18.95		
Keeping Score: An Inside Look at Sports Marketing	1-55571-377-7		☐ 18.95		
Know Your Market	1-55571-341-6 (B) ▪ 1-55571-333-5 (P)	☐ 39.95	☐ 19.95		
Leader's Guide: 15 Essential Skills	1-55571-434-X		☐ 19.95		
Legal Expense Defense	1-55571-349-1 (B) ▪ 1-55571-348-3 (P)	☐ 39.95	☐ 19.95		
Legal Road Map for Consultants	1-55571-460-9		☐ 18.95		
Location, Location, Location	1-55571-376-9		☐ 19.95		
Mail Order Legal Guide	1-55571-193-6 (B) ▪ 1-55571-190-1 (P)	☐ 45.00	☐ 29.95		
Managing People: A Practical Guide	1-55571-380-7		☐ 21.95		
Marketing for the New Millennium	1-55571-432-3		☐ 19.95		
Marketing Mastery	1-55571-358-0 (B) ▪ 1-55571-357-2 (P)	☐ 39.95	☐ 19.95		
Money Connection	1-55571-352-1 (B) ▪ 1-55571-351-3 (P)	☐ 39.95	☐ 24.95		
Moonlighting: Earning a Second Income at Home	1-55571-406-4		☐ 15.95		
Navigating the Marketplace: Growth Strategies for Small Business	1-55571-458-7		☐ 21.95		
No Money Down Financing for Franchising	1-55571-462-5		☐ 19.95		
Not Another Meeting!	1-55571-480-3		☐ 17.95		
People-Centered Profit Strategies	1-55571-517-6		☐ 18.95		

Sub-total for this side:

TITLE	ISBN	BINDER	PAPERBACK	QTY.	TOTAL
People Investment	1-55571-187-1 (B) ■ 1-55571-161-8 (P)	☐ 39.95	☐ 19.95		
Power Marketing for Small Business	1-55571-303-3 (B) ■ 1-55571-166-9 (P)	☐ 39.95	☐ 19.95		
Proposal Development	1-55571-067-0 (B) ■ 1-55571-431-5 (P)	☐ 39.95	☐ 21.95		
Prospecting for Gold	1-55571-483-8		☐ 14.95		
Public Relations Marketing	1-55571-459-5		☐ 19.95		
Raising Capital	1-55571-306-8 (B) ■ 1-55571-305-X (P)	☐ 39.95	☐ 19.95		
Renaissance 2000	1-55571-412-9		☐ 22.95		
Retail in Detail	1-55571-371-8		☐ 15.95		
The Rule Book of Business Plans for Startups	1-55571-519-2		☐ 18.95		
Secrets of High Ticket Selling	1-55571-436-6		☐ 19.95		
Secrets to Buying and Selling a Business	1-55571-489-7		☐ 24.95		
Secure Your Future	1-55571-335-1		☐ 19.95		
Selling Services	1-55571-461-7		☐ 18.95		
SmartStart Your (State) Business	varies per state		☐ 19.95		
Indicate which state you prefer:					
Small Business Insider's Guide to Bankers	1-55571-400-5		☐ 18.95		
Smile Training Isn't Enough	1-55571-422-6		☐ 19.95		
Start Your Business	1-55571-485-4		☐ 10.95		
Strategic Management for Small and Growing Firms	1-55571-465-X		☐ 24.95		
Successful Network Marketing	1-55571-350-5		☐ 15.95		
Surviving Success	1-55571-446-3		☐ 19.95		
TargetSmart!	1-55571-384-X		☐ 19.95		
Top Tax Saving Ideas for Today's Small Business	1-55571-463-3		☐ 16.95		
Truth About Teams	1-55571-482-X		☐ 18.95		
Twenty-One Sales in a Sale	1-55571-448-X		☐ 19.95		
WebWise	1-55571-501-X (B) ■ 1-55571-479-X (P)	☐ 29.95	☐ 19.95		
What's It Worth?	1-55571-504-4		☐ 22.95		
Which Business?	1-55571-390-4		☐ 18.95		
Write Your Own Business Contracts	1-55571-196-0 (B) ■ 1-55571-170-7 (P)	☐ 39.95	☐ 24.95		

Success Series	ISBN		PAPERBACK	QTY.	TOTAL
50 Ways to Get Promoted	1-55571-506-0		☐ 10.95		
You Can't Go Wrong By Doing It Right	1-55571-490-0		☐ 14.95		

Oasis Software	FORMAT	BINDER		QTY.	TOTAL
Company Policy Text Files	CD-ROM ☐		☐ 49.95		
Company Policy Text Files Book & Disk Package	CD-ROM ☐	☐ 89.95 (B)	☐ 69.95 (P)		
Financial Management Techniques Standalone	Floppy Disks ☐		☐ 99.95		
Financial Management Techniques Book & Disk Package	Floppy Disks ☐	☐ 129.95(B)	☐ 119.95(P)		
Insurance Assistant	Floppy Disks ☐		☐ 29.95		
Insurance Assistant & Buyer's Guide to Business Insurance	Floppy Disks ☐	☐ 59.95 (B)	☐ 39.95 (P)		
Winning Business Plans in Color CD-ROM	CD-ROM ☐		☐ 59.95		

Ordered by: *Please give street address*

NAME   TITLE

COMPANY

STREET ADDRESS

CITY   STATE   ZIP

DAYTIME PHONE   EMAIL

Ship to: *If different than above*

NAME   TITLE

COMPANY

STREET ADDRESS

CITY   STATE   ZIP

DAYTIME PHONE

Shipping:

YOUR ORDER IS:	ADD:
0-25	5.00
25.01-50	6.00
50.01-100	7.00
100.01-175	9.00
175.01-250	13.00
250.01-500	18.00
500.01+	4% of total

Subtotal from other side	
Subtotal from this side	
Shipping	
TOTAL	

PLEASE CALL FOR RUSH SERVICE OPTIONS.
INTERNATIONAL ORDERS, PLEASE CALL FOR A QUOTE ON CURRENT SHIPPING RATES.

Payment Method:
☐ CHECK   ☐ MONEY ORDER
☐ AMERICAN EXPRESS   ☐ DISCOVER
☐ MASTERCARD   ☐ VISA

CREDIT CARD NUMBER

EXPIRATION (MM/YY)   NAME ON CARD (PLEASE PRINT)

SIGNATURE OF CARDHOLDER (REQUIRED)

Fax this order form to: (541) 476-1479 or mail it to: P.O. Box 3727, Central Point, Oregon 97502
For more information about our products or to order online, visit http://www.psi-research.com

OASIS PRESS   BOOKS & SOFTWARE